The Islamic Empire

Don Nardo

LUCENT BOOKS

A part of Gale, Cengage Learning

Detroit • New York • San Francisco • New Haven, Conn • Waterville, Maine • London

LIBRARY OF CONGRESS CATALOGING-IN-PUBLICATION DATA

Nardo, Don, 1947-
  The Islamic Empire / by Don Nardo.
    p. cm. -- (World history)
  Includes bibliographical references and index.
  ISBN 978-1-4205-0634-1 (hardcover)
  1. Islamic Empire--Juvenile literature. 2. Islamic civilization--Juvenile literature. I. Title.
  DS38.3.N367 2011
  956'.01--dc22
                                                              2011016599

Lucent Books
27500 Drake Rd.
Farmington Hills, MI 48331

ISBN-13: 978-1-4205-0634-1
ISBN-10: 1-4205-0634-X

Printed in the United States of America
1 2 3 4 5 6 7 15 14 13 12 11

Printed by Bang Printing, Brainerd, MN, 1st Ptg., 08/2011

Contents

Foreword

Each year, on the first day of school, nearly every history teacher faces the task of explaining why his or her students should study history. Many reasons have been given. One is that lessons exist in the past from which contemporary society can benefit and learn. Another is that exploration of the past allows us to see the origins of our customs, ideas, and institutions. Concepts such as democracy, ethnic conflict, or even things as trivial as fashion or mores, have historical roots.

Reasons such as these impress few students, however. If anything, these explanations seem remote and dull to young minds. Yet history is anything but dull. And therein lies what is perhaps the most compelling reason for studying history: History is filled with great stories. The classic themes of literature and drama—love and sacrifice, hatred and revenge, injustice and betrayal, adversity and overcoming adversity—fill the pages of history books, feeding the imagination as well as any of the great works of fiction do.

The story of the Children's Crusade, for example, is one of the most tragic in history. In 1212 Crusader fever hit Europe. A call went out from the pope that all good Christians should journey to Jerusalem to drive out the hated Muslims and return the city to Christian control. Heeding the call, thousands of children made the journey. Parents bravely allowed many children to go, and entire communities were inspired by the faith of these small Crusaders. Unfortunately, many boarded ships were captained by slave traders, who enthusiastically sold the children into slavery as soon as they arrived at their destination. Thousands died from disease, exposure, and starvation on the long march across Europe to the Mediterranean Sea. Others perished at sea.

Another story, from a modern and more familiar place, offers a soul-wrenching view of personal humiliation but also the ability to rise above it. Hatsuye Egami was one of 110,000 Japanese Americans sent to internment camps during World War II. "Since yesterday we Japanese have ceased to be human beings," he wrote in his diary. "We are numbers. We are no longer Egamis, but the number 23324. A tag with that number is on every trunk, suitcase and bag. Tags, also, on our breasts." Despite such dehumanizing treatment, most internees worked hard to control their bitterness. They created workable communities inside the camps and demonstrated again and again their loyalty as Americans.

These are but two of the many stories from history that can be found in the pages of the Lucent Books World History series. All World History titles rely on sound research and verifiable evidence, and all give students a clear sense of time, place, and chronology through maps and timelines as well as text.

All titles include a wide range of authoritative perspectives that demonstrate the complexity of historical interpretation and sharpen the reader's critical thinking skills. Formally documented quotations and annotated bibliographies enable students to locate and evaluate sources, often instantaneously via the Internet, and serve as valuable tools for further research and debate.

Finally, Lucent's World History titles present rousing good stories, featuring vivid primary source quotations drawn from unique, sometimes obscure sources such as diaries, public records, and contemporary chronicles. In this way, the voices of participants and witnesses as well as important biographers and historians bring the study of history to life. As we are caught up in the lives of others, we are reminded that we too are characters in the ongoing human saga, and we are better prepared for our own roles.

Important Dates at the Time

476
The western sector of the Roman Empire falls; the eastern half, centered at Constantinople, survives.

622
Muhammad escapes from Mecca and travels to Medina, a journey later called the *Hijira*.

ca. 600
The Khmer Empire is established in Southeast Asia.

636
An Arab Muslim army scores a decisive victory over the Byzantines at Yarmouk, in Syria.

A.D. 500　　　610　　　620　　　630　　　640

630
In central Asia, the eastern Gokturk Empire collapses under the force of a Chinese invasion.

ca. 570
Muhammad, founder of the faith of Islam, is born in the Arabian city of Mecca.

632
By now called "the Prophet," Muhammad dies at the age of sixty-three.

ca. 650
Teotihuacán, in central Mexico, for over two centuries one of the world's largest cities, begins to decline.

610
Muhammad claims to have been visited by a supernatural being, later identified as the angel Gabriel.

of the Islamic Empire

656
Muhammad's cousin Ali wins a victory over his opponents in the so-called Battle of the Camel.

ca. 1000
Viking explorers become the first Europeans to land in North America.

1258
The Mongols capture Baghdad, ending both the Abbasid dynasty and medieval Islamic Empire.

ca. 711
After overrunning all of North Africa, Muslims cross the Strait of Gibraltar and land in Spain.

ca. 900
In Central America, the Mayan Empire mysteriously collapses.

650	700	750	1000	1500

732
Frankish war leader Charles Martel repulses a Muslim army near Tours, in central France.

750
The Umayyad dynasty is succeeded by the Abbasid line of rulers.

1415
England's King Henry V defeats the French at Agincourt.

661
After Ali's murder, Muawiya becomes caliph, initiating the Umayyad dynasty.

1453
The Ottoman Turks capture Constantinople, eradicating the Byzantine Empire.

Introduction

Dreams of Empires Lost

The phrase *the Islamic Empire* is often bandied about in both writing and conversation. (Some people call it the Muslim Empire. As a noun, the word *Muslim* means a follower of the faith of Islam, but as an adjective it is routinely used interchangeably with the word *Islamic*.) The problem is that to say *the* Muslim Empire is somewhat misleading. In reality, history has witnessed not just one such empire, but many. Indeed, between the early Middle Ages and the twentieth century, dozens of autocratic realms with Muslim leaders or dynasties and predominantly Muslim populations existed across the Middle East and elsewhere. (A dynasty is a family line of rulers.)

Nevertheless, historians and other writers often refer to the territories and rule of separate Muslim groups and dynasties during the early medieval period as *the* Islamic Empire, collectively. Usually this is done as a sort of historical shorthand, to indicate the predominant form of government or culture in the Middle East during that period. At its greatest extent, in fact, the area of Muslim-ruled territory stretched far beyond the Middle East. In the 600s and 700s A.D., Arab Muslim armies overran all of North Africa and even established a stronghold in southern Spain.

Scholars and others also frequently call the collective Muslim realms of the medieval period the Caliphate. That term derives from the word *caliph*, the title assumed by most of the leaders of the numerous medieval Islamic states. (The word *caliph* itself comes from the Arabic word *khalifa*, meaning "deputy").

Although the Caliphate, as a collective group of Islamic nations and societies, existed many centuries ago, it has highly significant relevance today. This is partly because some modern Muslims deplore the demise of the medieval Caliphate and yearn to see it someday revived. As King's College London scholar Efraim Karsh explains,

> The last great Muslim empire may have been destroyed and the Caliphate left vacant, but the Islamic imperial dream of world domination has remained very much alive in the hearts and minds of [some] Muslims. . . . This yearning for lost imperial dominions has by no means been confined to Asia. To this day, [some] Arabs and Muslims unabashedly pine for the restoration of Spain and consider their 1492 expulsion from that country a grave historical injustice.[1]

Rise of Radical Islam

It appears that only a small minority of modern Muslims seriously desire and expect the resurrection of some form of caliphate similar to the one that existed in the Middle Ages. Moreover, an even smaller minority within their ranks would resort to using force to bring such a restoration about. However, the few Muslims who *have* turned to violent means have made themselves virtual household names throughout the world. The various groups they have formed to carry out their militant agendas have most often come to be collectively called "radical Muslims," adherents of "radical Islam," or "Muslim terrorists" by their detractors.

The most infamous of these groups is al Qaeda, established by Osama bin Laden, who was born into a wealthy Saudi family. It was Bin Laden's organization that planned the attacks of September 11, 2001 (often called 9/11 for short), in which nineteen young Muslim men hijacked airliners. As people around the globe watched in horror, they crashed the planes into New York City's World Trade Center towers and Washington, DC's Pentagon building, killing nearly three thousand Americans. Almost ten years later Bin Laden paid a heavy price for these mass murders. In May 2011 he was killed by U.S. soldiers in a well-planned raid on his Pakistan hideout, an operation ordered and closely monitored by President Barack Obama. Nevertheless, though dealt a major blow, al Qaeda remained intact and a potential threat to Westerners and non-radical Muslims alike.

The rise of radical Islam, which actively seeks to create a new Islamic Empire as large or larger than the original one, occurred in the late twentieth century. Al Qaeda's own rise can be seen as a model for most other, similar groups with that overall aim. In 1979 Bin Laden, along with numerous other Muslims from various nations, went to Afghanistan to fight the Soviets, who had recently invaded that country. A few years later, while still battling the Soviets, Bin Laden established al Qaeda as a resistance group. When the invaders cut their losses and left Afghanistan the following year, Bin Laden and his followers decided to keep the organization going. Their goal was to fight for other causes in which they perceived that Muslims had been unfairly treated or oppressed.

Osama bin Laden founded the militant al Qaeda organization and helped to plan the group's September 11, 2001, terrorist attacks on the World Trade Center in New York City.

One such situation, from al Qaeda's point of view, was the 1991 entry of U.S. troops into Iraq. President George H. W. Bush sent them to free the tiny nation of Kuwait, which had been overrun a few months before by Iraq's brutal dictator Saddam Hussein. Bin Laden and his followers heartily disliked Saddam. But they even more bitterly resented the idea of American or other Western soldiers occupying soil they viewed as holy to all Muslims, lands that had once been part of the Caliphate.

From that time on, members of al Qaeda became convinced that the West, led by the United States, was out to beat down or even subjugate Muslim countries. Al Qaeda spokesmen routinely condemned Westerners, frequently suggesting that they had a secret agenda dedicated to keeping the Caliphate, or any collective Islamic movement or territory, from gaining strength. One such claim that al Qaeda trumpeted widely in the media stated,

> After the fall of our orthodox caliphates . . . our Islamic nation [meaning collective culture, or caliphate] was afflicted with [Western] rulers who took over in the Muslim nation. . . . Muslims have endured all kinds of harm, oppression, and torture at their hands. Those [rulers] did not stop there. They started to fragment the essence of the Islamic nation by trying to eradicate its Muslim identity. Thus, they started spreading godless and atheistic views among the youth. . . . Then [they began] using every means and [kind of] seduction, to produce a generation of young men that did not know [anything] except what [the rulers] want. . . . These young men realized that an Islamic government [ruling vast territories] would never be established except by the bomb and rifle. Islam does not coincide nor make a truce with

unbelief, but rather confronts it. . . . The young came to prepare themselves for Jihad [holy war]. [We] present this humble effort to these young Muslim men who are pure, believing, and fighting for the cause of Allah [God]. It is [our] contribution toward paving the road that . . . establishes a caliphate.[2]

Modern Civilization Challenged

The phrase "fighting for the cause of Allah" reveals the core rationale, or justification, cited by al Qaeda and other radical Islamic groups that employ aggressive means in hopes of restoring the Caliphate or something like it. They have committed many violent acts, including those perpetrated on 9/11, in the name of, and supposedly with the approval of, God. This notion—that God wants to see a vast Muslim Empire established—is actually not new. Many people in medieval times, even some non-Muslims, believed it.

One of these believers was a Christian monk named John bar Penkaye, who lived in Syria in the late 600s. Soon after Arab Muslim armies had created an enormous empire stretching across North Africa and the Middle East, he penned a chronicle describing these campaigns. How could men without armor, he asked,

> have been able to win, apart from divine aid, [and] bring low . . . the proud spirit of the Persians? Only a short period passed before the

entire world was handed over to the Arabs. They subdued all fortified cities, taking control from sea to sea [from the Atlantic Ocean in the west to the Indian Ocean in the east], and from east to west—Egypt [and] from [the Greek island of] Crete to Cappadocia [in what is now Turkey], from Yemen [in southern Arabia] to the gates of Alan [north of the Black Sea], Armenians, Syrians, Persians, Byzantines, and Egyptians, and all the areas in between. Their hand was upon everyone, as the Prophet [Muhammad] says.[3]

Clearly, Penkaye felt that it was impossible for these conquests to have occurred without some kind of "divine aid." So he concluded that Arab forces had conquered much of the known world because it was part of God's plan. That al Qaeda and other militant Muslim groups continue to believe this and to act on it is one of the major challenges presently facing modern civilization, especially in the West. One way that Westerners can combat the ongoing threat of radical Islam and its lingering dreams of empires lost is through knowledge. More specifically, by understanding how the medieval Caliphate was forged in the first place, the millions of people targeted by the radicals can better understand what they are up against.

Chapter One

Muhammad and His Struggles

The early medieval era witnessed one of the most momentous and memorable sequences of events in world history. In a series of swift and often irresistible waves, Arab Muslim armies swept out of the Arabian Peninsula and conquered most of the Middle East and North Africa. Beginning in the early 600s A.D., in only a century they had established a vast Islamic empire that stretched westward from Afghanistan, across the Middle East and North Africa, to Spain. Although a number of local rulers governed various sections of this huge realm, all of them proclaimed their allegiance to a central leader, the Caliph. Hence, the immense domain carved out by Muslim expansionists came to be called the Caliphate, or "dominion of the Caliph."

Even the Caliphs were not the supreme figures in the early Islamic Empire, however. Every one of these rulers owed his own allegiance, along with a profound political, cultural, and religious debt, to the Muslim community's founder and first leader. That individual was the Prophet Muhammad. Before dying in 632, he had brought most of Arabia into the Muslim fold, leaving the lion's share of the creation of the Caliphate to his immediate heirs. Because Muhammad initiated the Muslim conquests and established the Islamic faith, the extraordinary story of the medieval Islamic Empire begins with him.

The Early Medieval Superpowers

When Muhammad was born in Mecca, in western Arabia, in about 570, two large and powerful realms existed not far north of the Arab-controlled lands. One, the Byzantine Empire, was centered at Constantinople, a majestic city on the southern rim of the Black Sea. The last surviving portion of the Roman Empire, the western section of which

At the time of Muhammad's birth, the Byzantine Empire and the Persian Sassanian Empire were the two superpowers bordering the Arab world.

had collapsed a century before, the Byzantine Empire was a proudly Christian state. In the late 500s the Greek-speaking Byzantines lorded over expansive territories, including Greece, Italy, Anatolia (what is now Turkey), Palestine, and large sections of North Africa.

The other major realm the Arabs contended with in the north was the Sassanian (or Sassanid) Empire. Modeled on the old Persian Empire, which the legendary Greek conqueror Alexander the Great had captured some nine centuries before, the Sassanian state kept alive the faith of the ancient Persian monarchs—Zoroastrianism. This set of beliefs had been established in the dim past by a prophet named Zarathushtra (called Zoroaster by the Greeks). Zoroastrianism was more or less a monotheistic belief system featuring a supreme god known as Ahura-Mazda (the "wise lord"). When Muhammad was born, the Sassanian Empire was at its height, encompassing what are now Iraq, Iran, Armenia, and Afghanistan.

None of the peoples who lived along the fringes of these two enormous realms could match them in size, population, wealth, or military power. Indeed, the Byzantine and Sassanian states were in a very real sense the superpowers of their day. "Together," scholars Fred J. Hill and Nicholas Awde point out,

> they dominated a huge swathe of territory [that stretched] from Eastern Europe across the Middle East and into parts of central Asia [and] encompassed some of the greatest trade routes of the day.... Continuously at odds with each other, the two superpowers vied for control of the surrounding regions and their lucrative trade routes. This they did either by brute force or by expertly exploiting local regions and ethnic rivalries. Caught up in the struggle for economic supremacy was the region of Arabia [the Arabian Peninsula].[4]

The Arabian Peninsula and Mecca

Although less numerous, organized, wealthy, and powerful than their neighbors to the north, the Arabs were nevertheless hardworking and ambitious. At the time, a majority of Arabia's residents lived near its coasts. The coastal regions were more fertile and livable than the interior, which was largely made up of extremely arid deserts. Some Arabs were still nomads, known as bedouins. They tended to move from place to place, seeking suitable places to graze their livestock.

However, by the time Muhammad was a child, large numbers of Arabs, including his own relatives, had become city dwellers. They lived in prosperous towns in the more watered regions and participated in vigorous trade, not only with one another but also with regions to the east and west of Arabia. Initially, the most prominent of these towns were Saba, Hadramawt, Qataban, and Ma'in, all situated in the peninsula's southwestern sector, which enjoyed more rain than other areas. Washington State University scholar Richard Hooker describes this commerce and its significance for the Arabs' future:

> The most powerful of all these [southern] city-states was Saba, which [was located] on two major trade routes. One was the ocean-trading route between Africa and India. The harbors of the southwest were centers of commerce with these two continents and the luxury items, such as spices, imported from these countries. But the Sabaean region also lay at the southern terminus [end] of land-based trade routes [running] up and down the coast of the Arabian peninsula. Goods would travel down this land-route to be exported to Africa or India and goods from Africa and India would travel north on this land-route. This latter trade route had tremendous consequences for the Arabs in the north and the subsequent history of Islam. For all along this trade route grew major trading cities and the wealth of the south filtered north into these cities. It was in one such Arabian city, Mecca, that Islam would begin.[5]

In addition to their extensive trade with towns and kingdoms lying to their south, west, and east, the Meccans looked for opportunities in the empires far to the north. The city's merchants "had commercial relations with both Persians [Sassanians] and Byzantines and sent caravans twice yearly to the north," historian Alfred Guillaume remarks. "The Quraysh, the tribe to which Muhammad belonged, formed companies which shared in the profits of these ventures." The dominant posi-

tion of traders in Meccan society was demonstrated by the fact that "the town itself was governed by a committee of prominent merchants called the *mala*."[6]

Early medieval Mecca became not only a leading trading hub in western Arabia but also one of the peninsula's chief religious centers. Most pre-Islamic Arabs were polytheistic, meaning they worshipped multiple gods. Some of these deities were local and venerated in specific regions or by individual tribes, while others were recognized through-

Located on the Arabian Peninsula, the ancient city of Saba was an important trade-route center during Muhammad's time.

out the peninsula. Of the latter, the most important was a sort of supreme god called Allah. (Versions of the name Allah existed in other Semitic languages beside Arabic. In ancient Hebrew writings, for example, God was often referred to as Elohim, a plural form of *Eloah*, more or less equivalent to the Arabic *Allah*.) The daughters of the pre-Islamic Allah were the popular Arabian goddesses Manat, Al-Lat, and Al-Uzza.

Members of different Arabian religious persuasions did not try to deny the existence of one another's gods. Rather, the general consensus was that all of these divinities existed, and there was an annual pilgrimage from far and wide to Mecca to pay them collective respect. Known as the hajj, it was a custom that the Muslims would later adapt to fit their own needs. Worshippers taking part in a pre-Islamic hajj converged at a large cube-shaped building called the Kaaba. There, likely where a meteorite (a rock from outer space) had landed long before, figurines and statues of the various gods were set up. Like tourists in all places and times, the pilgrims who came to pray to these idols were subject to the commercial exploitation of the locals. The Quraysh earned extra money by charging fees to those who desired to see the divine images.

Arabian deities, however, were not the only ones worshipped in western and northern Arabia. That region had become a cultural and religious melting pot where people from foreign lands had settled in preceding centuries. Among them were monotheists, includ-

Many Arabian religions participated in the hajj, a pilgrimage to Mecca. The goal of the pilgrims' journey was to visit the Kaaba (depicted here), a small building that houses a sacred stone.

ing Jews, Christians, and Zoroastrian Persians. Thus, the early medieval Arabs were already exposed to the concept of a single, solitary god. Possibly, that first-hand contact with Jews and Christians had already begun to make Muhammad doubt the local polytheistic belief system even before he had the first of his famous heavenly visions.

The Making of a Prophet

According to tradition, the first of those visions, which were destined to change the course of history, took place in 610, when Muhammad, whose name means "worthy of praise," was forty. Very little is known about his life up to that time. Among the few facts pieced together by later historians are that he was a merchant and a member of the Quraysh tribe's Hashim clan. Also, his father died before he was born, and his mother passed away when he was six, so the boy's paternal grandfather, Abdul Muttalib, raised him as his own. Muttalib himself died just two years later, at which point Muhammad came under the protective wing of his uncle, Abu Talib. Eventually, according to most accounts, the young man followed the example of a majority of his male relatives and became a merchant. Then, when he was perhaps twenty-five, he married a woman fifteen years his senior—Khadija. She gave him six children, two of whom died in childhood. (The four survivors were daughters Fatima, Zaynab, Umm Kulthum, and Ruqayya.)

The fantastic vision and revelation that changed Muhammad's life happened during a trip he took into the countryside. As several other Meccan men did, on occasion he went out alone to rest and meditate.

On one occasion, on a slope of Mount Hira, not far from Mecca, he found a cave spacious enough to shelter him from the elements. There he lay down and went to sleep. Guillaume tells what tradition says happened next:

The angel Gabriel [who did not identify himself] came to see him with a piece of silk brocade [on which] words were written, and said "Recite!" [Muhammad] answered, "What shall I recite?" The order was repeated three times, while he felt increasing physical pressure, until the angel said: "Recite in the name of your Lord who created man from [a] blood [clot]. Recite! Your Lord is wondrous kind, who by the pen has taught mankind things they knew not [as they were blind to them]." When [Muhammad] awoke, these words seemed to be written on his heart, or, as we should say, impressed indelibly [permanently] on his mind. . . . While he was on his way [home] he heard a voice from heaven hailing him as the Apostle of God.[7]

When Muhammad arrived at his house, he told Khadija what had occurred. Still trembling, he speculated that the spirit he had encountered might be some kind of demon or other evil creature. But such scary thoughts melted away when the strange celestial visitor paid him another visit. Identifying itself as the angel Gabriel, it said that Muhammad was Allah's prophet, or messenger, and once more commanded that he

A sixteenth-century illuminated manuscript depicts Muhammad's vision of the angel Gabriel.

طانق دوقلدم نكم الله تعالى باكه امراندى يبرنه كوزدمرسم
داخ يبريوزند نكاح اتكل بتول عذراى فاطمة الزهراى
على برله ولندركدى اندن جبرايلينه كوكه اعدى

اولدم امير المؤمنين على المرتضى مسلمه اوند رسول خذمتنه

recite. Again Muhammad asked what it was that he should say. This time the visitor reached out and squeezed him, after which Muhammad started speaking words that seemed to flow from his mouth without his even thinking them. Clearly, he conjectured, these words must be coming from God.

In the months and years that followed, the uncanny being calling itself Gabriel paid Muhammad many more visits, and each time Muhammad uttered a few more sentences that appeared to stream into him from a divine source. Muhammad did not jot down these words each time. This was because he, like many other Arabs of his day, was illiterate. Instead, he told the words to several companions, who memorized them and in turn told them to scribes. The latter wrote the words down on both stone tablets and the wide fronds of date palms. Eventually, all of the words and sentences added up to a book-length document that came to be known as the sacred Quran (or Qur'an or Koran). That word means "recitation" in Arabic. The book features a total of 114 chapters (suras), which break down into 6,236 verses (ayat).

Muhammad and his companions saw that the Quran contained many specific ideas, statements, and principles. Among them were religious doctrines and laws, as well as guidelines for decent human conduct, a just society, and a fair economic system. But overall, a few main, sweeping, and potent themes emerged. One was that the numerous gods that most Arabs had long accept-ed were false and that there exists but a single, supreme god—Allah. Another major theme was that all people need to totally surrender, or submit, to the will of Allah. That concept was strongly emphasized in the new faith's name—Islam, roughly translated as "surrender" or "submission" to God. Another important concept of the Quran pertained to Muhammad himself. One line reads: "Muhammad is not the father of any of your men, but he is the Apostle of Allah and the last of the prophets."[8] That made it clear that Muhammad was the last of a long line of prophets. These include several recognized by Jews and Christians, too, among them Adam, Abraham, Moses, and Jesus.

Cruel Persecutions and the Hijira

The first converts to the new faith Muhammad believed had been established by God's will were his wife, Khadija; his ten-year-old cousin Ali; his adopted son Zaid; and his trusted friend Abu Bakr. Over time, the Prophet, as Muhammad came to be known, and the initial converts convinced several other Meccans to become Muslims, or followers of Islam. Eventually, however, some of the town's leaders got wind of what was happening. They did not mind that the Muslims worshipped Allah, since that deity was revered by all Arabs. But the leaders were disturbed to hear Muhammad and his followers repeatedly saying that the other gods worshipped at the Kaaba were false. On the one hand, this seemed like sacrilege. On

Islam's Five Pillars

The so-called Five Pillars of Islam developed during Muhammad's own lifetime. Sunni Muslims came to perform them as described here, while Shia Muslims carry them out with a few minor differences. First there is a statement of belief, called the *shahadah*. Essentially, it states that no other gods but Allah (the deity worshipped by the Muslims, Jews, and Christians) exist and that Muhammad is God's last prophet. The second pillar, *salah* in Arabic, is the act of praying to God five times each day. Where the situation warrants, the muezzin, an official in a nearby mosque, calls the faithful to prayer and during that act they kneel down and face in the direction of Mecca. The third of Islam's five customary rituals, the *zakat*, consists of giving charity to poorer, less fortunate individuals in one's society. Muslims who are particularly financially well-off are expected to be especially generous. The fourth pillar, called *sawm*, is the practice of fasting from sunup to sundown during the sacred month of Ramadan. (A minority of Muslims fast during other months.) The fifth and last pillar of the faith is the hajj, consisting of a trip to Mecca at least once in a person's lifetime. There, the visitors circle the holy Kaaba (a cube-shaped monument thought to have been originally constructed by the patriarch Abraham) seven times.

the other, if those gods ceased to be worshipped, the leaders would no longer be able to collect the fees they charged religious pilgrims to visit the Kaaba. In addition, Muhammad's claim to religious authority openly challenged the social and religious authority of the elite men who ran the community.

As a result, those men condemned the Muslims and urged any and all Meccans to persecute them. Threatened and sometimes even assaulted, a number of Muhammad's followers, including his daughter Ruqayya, fled the town. Muhammad, Khadija, and about seventy others stayed in Mecca, hoping to convince their detractors to halt the persecutions. These efforts failed, however. What is more, Muhammad's personal misery increased when two of his closest relations—Khadija and Abu Talib—died in 619.

In the two years that followed, the persecution of Muslims in Mecca became so intense that the Prophet feared his people might be murdered. To forestall such a disaster, early in 622 he decided to send them all away to a safer place. Only Abu Bakr, who refused to leave his side, remained. Yathrib, situated about 215 miles (350km) north of Mecca, was chosen, partly because its residents had already invited Muhammad to visit or move there. One modern scholar

describes Yathrib as "a well-watered desert oasis on the merchant route to Syria."[9] He adds that the town had originally been settled by Jewish refugees fleeing Roman persecution.

> Their thriving farming and commercial enterprises attracted a substantial number of pagan Arabs to the site, [who] dominated the Jews yet remained torn by internal strife. The invitation to come to Yathrib as a peacemaker, made by representatives of the feuding tribes, thus provided Muhammad with a golden opportunity for spiritual and political pre-eminence, which he did not fail to seize.[10]

Once he was sure that the members of his flock were safe, Muhammad prepared for his own departure. Hearing that he and Abu Bakr had been targeted by some local assassins, after dark on July 16, 622, the two men escaped Mecca and headed north with the assassins in hot pursuit. Managing to evade these would-be killers, Muhammad and Abu Bakr eventually made it to Yathrib. Their fateful flight to that town was thereafter called the *Hijira* (or Hegira). It became a milestone in Islamic history and lore, partly because it ensured that the faith

This manuscript depicts Muhammad and his cousin Ali removing idols from the Kaaba in Mecca. Fearing persecution, Muhammad and his followers fled to the town of Yathrib.

would survive and also because saving the community from certain death transformed Muhammad into a political and military leader as well as a religious one. Not long after he arrived in Yathrib and helped the residents to solve their local dispute, the town was renamed Medina (the English version of an Arabic name meaning "City of the Prophet").

Medina turned out to be a fortunate place for the Muslims to live. The townspeople, with their mix of Jewish and Arab backgrounds, were friendly and religiously tolerant. That allowed Islam to prosper there, as well as with the inhabitants of the surrounding region. Noted American historian W. H. McNeill explains why the new faith appealed so much to these early Arabs. It had a high degree of "theological simplicity," he says. The Quran called for five straightforward, simple, easy-to-fulfill obligations expected of a Muslim. Later called Islam's "Five Pillars," they included: the acknowledgment that there is no god but Allah; praying to Allah five times each day; fasting during one month each year; giving charity to the poor; and visiting Mecca and the Kaaba at least once in one's lifetime. This uncomplicated approach to faith, McNeill continues,

> appealed to those Arabs who had abandoned the nomadic way of life for agriculture or trading, and who found difficulty in adjusting traditional tribal [religious] customs to the necessities of their new style of life. Judaism and to a

The Medina Charter

The Constitution of Medina, sometimes called the Medina Charter, made between Muhammad and the people of Medina in 622, says in part:

This is a document from Muhammad the Prophet (governing the relations) between the believers and Muslims . . . and those who followed them and joined them and labored with them. They are one community (umma) to the exclusion of all men. . . . The God-fearing believers shall be against the rebellious or him who seeks to spread injustice, or sin, or animosity, or corruption between believers. . . . A believer shall not slay a believer for the sake of an unbeliever, nor shall he aid an unbeliever against a believer. . . . Believers are friends one to the other to the exclusion of outsiders. To the Jew who follows us belong help and equality. He shall not be wronged nor shall his enemies be aided. The peace of the believers is indivisible. . . . Conditions must be fair and equitable to all. . . . Yathrib [Medina] shall be a sanctuary for the people of this document. A stranger under protection shall be as his host doing no harm and committing no crime. . . . If any dispute or controversy likely to cause trouble should arise it must be referred to God and to Muhammad the apostle of God.

Quoted in Alfred Guillaume, ed. and trans. *The Life of Muhammad.* New York: Oxford University Press, 1955, pp. 231–233.

Muhammad explains the document later called the Constitution of Medina to his followers in Yathrib.

lesser degree Christianity also had begun to move into this vacuum in the Arab community. . . . But Arab pride resisted the acceptance of a foreign faith. Muhammad's revelation, specially attuned to urban living and addressed specifically to Arabs . . . therefore met a definite need among a small but strategically situated portion of the Arab population.[11]

A Religious Revolution

Recognizing that Islam, with its simplicity and basic appeal, neatly filled this spiritual void in Arab society, Muhammad brilliantly took a series of steps to ensure the faith would take firm root and steadily spread. First, he had a document later called the Constitution of Medina drawn up. An agreement between the members of the Muslim community, or *umma* (or *ummah*), and the Prophet himself, it asked for all members to pay taxes to support that community. It also granted religious freedom for Jews and members of other faiths. In addition, Muhammad initiated a new custom relating to prayer. It specified that when worshippers prayed, they should face in the direction of Mecca, the site of the Kaaba, which was still holy to Allah.

Muhammad also took advantage of his new image as the military commander of the new faith. Believing that the Meccans would sooner or later attack Medina in an effort to wipe out the Muslim community, he decided to strike first. In 624 he ordered an assault on a merchants' caravan, guarded by a small army of Meccan fighters, that was traveling from Mecca to Syria. Taken by surprise, the Meccans were roundly defeated.

Less than a year later, the embarrassed Meccan leaders ordered a counterattack. In March 625, in a valley near Mount Uhud in northwestern Arabia, about thirty-two hundred Meccans met a group of roughly seven hundred Muslims in a small but bloody pitched battle. Muhammad's followers were forced to retreat. Then, in 627 the Meccans laid siege to Medina for forty days. When this militant move failed miserably, thanks to an inventive defensive strategy engineered by Muhammad himself, the Meccans lost face with Arabs across the peninsula. This allowed the Prophet to negotiate a treaty with the enemy.

The treaty proved to be another turning point in Islam's struggle for acceptance. The Meccans reluctantly agreed to allow Muslims to enter their town and visit the Kaaba. Just as Muhammad anticipated, gaining access to Mecca proved a crucial advantage because his followers now had a chance to talk to and convert the residents. That conversion progressed so rapidly that in 629 the Muslims managed to take charge of Mecca without resorting to violence. At Muhammad's order, the statues of the old Arabic gods were removed from the Kaaba.

Not long after this triumph for Islam, the faith encountered yet another unexpected turn of events, this one tragic.

Attack at Dawn

Early Muslim poets sometimes captured the martial, or military-oriented, aspects of life in their region, where nearly all able-bodied men doubled as soldiers, and squabbles between tribes were commonplace. This poem, ascribed to al-Tufayl, a contemporary of the Prophet Muhammad, describes an attack by the poet's tribe on a rival group.

We came upon them at dawn with our tall steeds, lean and sinewy, and spears whose steel was as burning flame. And swords that reap the necks, keen and sharp of edge, kept carefully in the sheaths until time of need. . . . We came upon their host in the morning, and they were like a flock of sheep on who falls the ravening wolf. . . . We fell on them with white steel ground to keenness. We cut them to pieces until they were destroyed. And we carried off their women on the saddles behind us, with their cheeks bleeding, torn in anguish by their nails.

Quoted in Hugh Kennedy. *The Great Arab Conquests: How the Spread of Islam Changed the World We Live In.* Cambridge, MA: Da Capo, 2008, p. 41.

On June 8, 632, Muhammad died in Medina at age sixty-three. The precise cause of his demise remains uncertain, but based on the symptoms described by his followers some modern doctors say it might have been bacterial meningitis.

Although Abu Bakr and other leading Muslims were deeply saddened by their leader's passing, they did not despair for the new faith he had created. Indeed, they seemed to sense that Muhammad had laid a sturdy foundation for others to build on. Their positive feelings that their beliefs would steadily spread across all of Arabia were soon borne out.

In the words of an expert on the Islamic Empire, David Nicolle,

> Out of [the diverse] peoples of Arabia, with contrasting ways of life and different languages, would emerge a religious revolution. . . . For the first time in recorded history, the Arabs [had been] united by an indigenous [local] leader, inspired by their own ideology. With the coming of Muhammad, a unifying religious force was created for the region, which fueled the conquest of not only Arabia itself, but lands and hearts far beyond.[12]

Chapter Two

The Early Muslim Conquests

Not long after Muhammad's death in 632, the followers of his new faith, Islam, swept out of Arabia and began absorbing enormous tracts of territory. The culture of the conquerors strongly impacted these many lands and peoples. Although the Muslims did not force their religion on the subdued populations, over time most of the inhabitants converted on their own. The overall result was that these peoples were profoundly transformed, and most of them remain Muslim today, more than thirteen centuries later.

One of the driving forces behind this mighty burst of imperialistic expansion, one of the biggest in world history, was a concept best known by the Arabic term *jihad*. The original and literal meaning of the word is "struggle," usually in the sense of striving for a cause or a personal goal. Many such causes were and remain worthy and nonviolent. A person who tries hard to achieve moral excellence, for example, and a group that fights to gain lost freedom can both be said to be performing jihad.

On occasion, however, Muslims have applied the concept of jihad to warfare, often referred to as "holy war" in the West. This was the way the term was frequently used in the 600s and 700s, when Arab armies were almost constantly on the offensive. Many of the soldiers fought mainly for money or other valuables they could plunder. But others used certain phrases in the Quran to justify these naked conquests, similar to the way Christian zealots have sometimes used statements from the Bible to rationalize various crimes and bad behavior.

One such Quranic text, plainly aimed at those who had attacked Muhammad and his followers, reads: "Will you not fight a people who broke their oaths and

Spread of the Islamic Empire

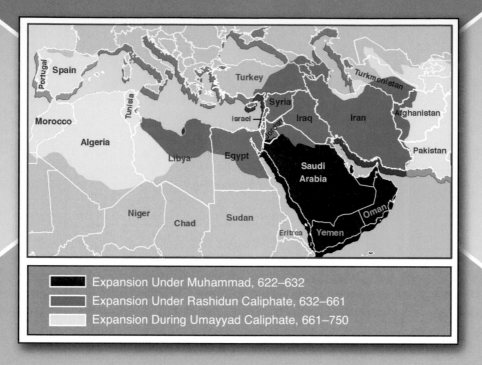

Expansion Under Muhammad, 622–632
Expansion Under Rashidun Caliphate, 632–661
Expansion During Umayyad Caliphate, 661–750

Taken from: Wikipedia Commons.

aimed at the expulsion of the Apostle [i.e., Muhammad], and they attacked you first? . . . Fight them, [for] Allah will punish them by your hands and bring them to disgrace." Another passage was used to justify making war on "idolaters," or people who worshipped idols (statues of various deities): "Slay the idolaters wherever you find them, and take them captives and besiege them. . . . If they repent [give up their false religion] . . . leave [them alone, for] surely Allah is forgiving."[13] James E. Lindsay, a historian at Colorado State University, elaborates:

After Muhammad's death, his followers used these texts and others like them to form the basis for an ideology of jihad in the medieval Islamic world. They inspired many of the faithful during the Islamic conquests of the seventh century, even as others were undoubtedly inspired merely by booty and glory in battle. Once the frontiers of the new Islamic empire were more or less stabilized . . . the caliphs maintained an expansionist jihad ideology by leading or ordering raids along the [empire's borders].[14]

The Succession

Before they could debate concepts such as ideology and expansion, however, Muhammad's followers needed to deal with the trauma of his passing. First, he was so beloved by them that most were beside themselves with grief, and some were downright poetic in their eulogies for him. His cousin Ali, for example, said in part,

> You gave a message of hope to the people. You showed them the right path. You established a new order. You are the savior of humankind. You established equality among the people. You ushered in a revolution. . . . You will guide us even after death. . . . From God you came and to God you have returned. May your soul rest in peace close to your creator.[15]

That Muhammad would continue to "guide" his followers "even after death," as Ali said, was true enough religiously speaking. Politically speaking was another matter, however. The faithful needed to choose someone to replace Muhammad as leader of the *umma*, but he had failed to leave behind either the name of his heir or a specific procedure for choosing a successor. As the late English historian Albert Hourani put it,

> When Muhammad died, there was a moment of confusion among his followers. [There was] a role to be filled, that of arbiter of disputes and maker of decisions within

the community. There were three main groups among the followers of Muhammad: the early companions who had made the hijira with him, a group linked [to him and one another] by intermarriage; the prominent men of Medina who had made the compact [constitution] with him there; and the members of the leading Meccan families, mainly of recent conversion.[16]

At a meeting of representatives from these groups, a member of the first—Abu Bakr, who had fled with the Prophet from Mecca to Medina in 622—was

This illuminated manuscript depicts Muhammad with his cousin Ali and the future first caliph, Abu Bakr.

selected as the new head of the umma. In addition to being Muhammad's close friend, Abu Bakr was also his father-in-law, as the Prophet had married Abu Bakr's daughter, Aisha, in 623. These intimate connections with Muhammad satisfied most, though certainly not all, of the faithful. (The Muslims who disagreed with this choice would later loudly make their case.) Those who had chosen Abu Bakr conferred on him the title of Caliph, after which he rather humbly told them,

O people, I have been appointed to rule over you, though I am not the best among you. If I do well, help me, and if I do ill, correct me. Truth is loyalty and falsehood is treachery. The weak among you is strong in my eyes until I get justice for him, please God, and the strong among you is weak in my eyes until I exact justice from him, please God.[17]

The First Caliph

In the same speech, Abu Bakr proceeded to set the stage for the conquests and expansion in which large numbers of Muslims were about to become involved. "If any people hold back from fighting the holy war for God," he declared, "God strikes them with degradation. If weakness spreads among a people, God brings disaster upon all of them."[18] Exactly what Abu Bakr meant by "holy war" at that moment remains unclear. Possibly, he was speaking in a general or metaphoric

sense to emphasize that Muslims should and would be ready to fight against any and all enemies of Allah and the *umma*.

Even if the latter interpretation is correct, Abu Bakr and his followers were soon embroiled in a series of very real wars and military expeditions. The first occurred only a few weeks after he had accepted the office of Caliph. Many of the Arab bedouins whom Muhammad had earlier convinced to join the Muslim community, broke with the *umma* following the Prophet's passing. Abu Bakr labeled their departure an insurrection and apostasy (rejection of one's former religion). Because the Arabic word for apostasy is *ridda*, the battles against the bedouins became known as the Ridda wars. Abu Bakr and his followers took a bit less than a year to defeat the rebellious tribes and bring all of Arabia back into the Muslim fold.

It appears that Abu Bakr and his chief advisers learned a valuable lesson from the Ridda wars. This was that they had no way of knowing when and how uprisings or other attacks on the Muslim community might occur in the future. In fact, now that Arabia had been united under strong, bold military forces, that region might well be seen as a threat in the eyes of neighboring states, especially the Sassanian and Byzantine Empires. Perhaps, Abu Bakr reasoned, one of those outside powers might contemplate delivering a preemptive strike designed to nip Arabic aspirations in the bud.

Rather than wait for such a foreign attack to materialize, the recently

Prophets of the People of the Book

Islam recognizes a number of early prophets, among them many of the same ones revered by Christians and Jews. This small excerpt from the Quran mentions several of the major Islamic prophets (outside of Muhammad himself) and makes the point that a single deity oversees all three faiths, each of which traces its origins back to Abraham.

Ours is the community of Abraham, a man of pure worship. No polytheist he! Let your word be: "We believe in God and in what has been revealed to us, and revealed to Abraham, Ishmael, Isaac, Jacob, and the tribes, and we believe in what was brought to Moses, to Jesus, and to the [other] prophets, from their Lord. We do not distinguish between any of them and to God we make submission. . . . People of the Book [i.e., Jews, Christians, and Muslims] do not go unwarranted lengths [and] get involved in false utterances relating to God. . . . Do not talk of three gods. You are well advised to abandon such ideas. Truly God is one God [over everyone].

Quran, sura 2. Quoted in Marven Gettleman and Stuart Schaar, eds. *The Middle East and Islamic World Reader*. New York: Grove, 2003, p. 15.

A sixteenth-century illuminated manuscript depicts Muhammad with Moses and the Archangel Gabriel. Muhammad said that a single deity oversees all three faiths: Judaism, Christianity, and Islam.

appointed Caliph decided to strike the first blow. In 633 he sent small but ardent and capable bands of fighters into Iraq and Palestine, where they captured several towns. Following this aggression, Abu Bakr fully realized, the Byzantines and Sassanians would retaliate. However, he was confident that the Muslims had a number of advantages in the coming conflicts. First, the two great empires to the north were militarily exhausted after generations of fighting each other, so any forces they sent southward to deal with the Arab incursions would likely be of second-rate quality, as well as unsuspecting of the tremendous effectiveness of the Arab fighters.

An even more important advantage the Arabs possessed at the time was their zeal to fight, based partly on their strong belief that their cause was just. Indeed, the general consensus among them was that their community must be protected and defended at all costs. The late, noted German historian Theodor Noeldeke suggested an added dimension—the perceived need to use the fervor for conquest as a way to maintain the recently created enthusiasm and momentum of the *umma* itself. In his words,

It was certainly good policy to turn the recently subdued tribes of the wilderness towards an external aim, in which they might at once satisfy their lust for booty on a grand scale, maintain their warlike feeling, and strengthen themselves in their attachment to the new faith. . . . Muhammad himself had already sent expeditions across the [Byzantine] frontier, and thereby had pointed out the way to his successors. To follow in his footsteps was in accordance with the innermost being of the youthful Islam, already grown great amid the tumult of arms.[19]

Noeldeke's view remains somewhat controversial among experts. Whether he was correct or not, undoubtedly the early Muslim conquerors were filled with a passion for expanding the *umma* and the power base of its leaders. There was "an unwavering feeling of supremacy and buoyant conviction in its ultimate triumph," Efraim Karsh writes. This eagerness for expansion filled the early Muslims "with the necessary sense of purpose, self-confidence, and revolutionary zeal to take on the region's established empires." Whether the conquests were initiated by small raiding parties acting on their own or by a grand plan of the caliphs, Karsh adds, "is immaterial. Empires are born of chance as well as design. What counts is that the Arab conquerors acted in a typically imperialist fashion from the start, subjugating [overpowering] indigenous populations."[20]

The Conquests of Umar

Although Abu Bakr set the conflicts with the Byzantine and Sassanian realms in motion, he died in 634, before most of the main fighting took place. He was succeeded by another friend and father-in-law of the Prophet, Umar ibn al-Khattab. Under the second caliph, Muslim

The brilliant strategist Khalid ibn al-Walid, right, on horse, defeated the Byzantines at the battle of Yarmouk in A.D. 636.

forces significantly increased the size and intensity of their campaigns against Byzantine and Sassanian holdings in the Middle East. In the eight years following Umar's assumption of power, his soldiers seized a huge amount of territory. It included Byzantine-controlled southern Syria, along with the major Syrian city of Damascus.

The most strategic event in the fight for Syria was the battle of Yarmouk, in 636. The Muslim forces were led by Abu Ubaidah, who was advised by the brilliant military leader Khalid ibn al-Walid,

Umar's cousin. The following account of the battle is by University of St. Andrews scholar Hugh Kennedy. After several days of minor skirmishes, Kennedy says,

the real fighting began when the Muslims feigned [pretended] a retreat from their positions and lured elements of the Byzantine army into rough terrain, where they were ambushed. During the [battle] the Byzantine cavalry [mounted fighters] became separated from the infantry [foot soldiers], enabling the Muslim cavalry to inflict great slaughter. . . . The main Byzantine force was now driven west and hemmed in between the rugged valleys [near] the cliffs of the Yarmouk gorge. [Muslim] forces went on to storm the Byzantine camp, [where] morale broke and the Byzantine forces lost all cohesion. There are reports of exhausted and dejected soldiers sitting down [and] waiting for death. Others were driven down the cliffs into the wadis [dried up riverbeds]. The Muslims took very few prisoners.[21]

After southern Syria had been absorbed, Umar's armies went on to take other Byzantine-controlled areas. Among them were northern Syria, Jerusalem and surrounding regions in Palestine, and Egypt. The Muslims also captured Iraq (Mesopotamia), then a major portion of the Sassanian heartland. Soon the whole Sassanian Empire collapsed under the impact of the Arab invasion.

While these attacks were taking place, Umar developed a military-political policy for the conquered lands that was destined to remain in effect for many decades to come. At Umar's orders, Hourani explains,

the conquerors exercised their authority from armed camps where the Arabian soldiers were placed. In Syria, these for the most part lay in the cities which already existed, but elsewhere new settlements were made, [in] Basra and Kufa in Iraq, Fustat in Egypt (from which Cairo was later to grow), [and] others. . . . Being centers of power, these camps were poles of attraction for immigrants from Arabia and the conquered lands, and they grew into cities, with the governor's palace and the place of public assembly, the mosque, at the center.[22]

Keeping most of the Arab soldiers in these settlements, a practice that continued for many years to come, had crucial consequences. First, the vast majority of these fighters did not settle down and become merchants or farmers in the conquered lands. So the natives retained most of their lands and their traditional cultures as well. That lenient policy made many of them less likely to revolt against their new overlords. Also, the caliphs had the advantage of keeping most of their soldiers in almost full military mode, ready to launch new conquests at the ruler's order.

The Early Conversions

Contrary to an assertion often mistakenly made in Western media and writings, the early Muslim armies did not force the residents of the conquered lands to convert to Islam. British historian Malise Ruthven explains here how these conversions came about.

The process of Islamization [conversion to Islam] occurred gradually, through marriage, as the leading families of the subject populations sought to join the Muslim elites. It also occurred as impoverished or uprooted subjects found support in the religion of their rulers, or as people disenchanted with their former rulers found a congenial spiritual home in one that honored their traditions. . . . The role of early Muslim missionaries was also crucial in the process. [Finally] Islam carried with it the prestige of learning and literacy into illiterate cultures. . . . The prestige of literacy, symbolized by the [often beautifully illustrated] Quran, [was] powerful. Even Mongol invaders, notorious for their cruelty, would succumb to the spiritual and aesthetic power of Islam in the western part of their dominions.

Malise Ruthven. *Historical Atlas of Islam*. Cambridge, MA: Harvard University Press, 2004, pp. 10–11.

Another key aspect of Umar's political policy for the conquered territories was related to the restraint and moderation he used in dealing with the inhabitants of these lands. Their retention of their time-honored customs included their religious beliefs. A sinister myth that spread through Western countries over the centuries is that the medieval Muslim conquerors forced the peoples they defeated to convert to Islam. The reality was that most residents of these areas enjoyed religious toleration. In particular, the Muslims respected the beliefs of Jews and Christians, whom they viewed as part of their own religious family. In Islamic tradition, Christians, Jews, and

Muslims are all descended from the biblical patriarch Abraham and his sons and together make up the so-called *ahl al-kitab*, or "people of the book." Moreover, David Nicolle writes,

forcible conversion is specifically banned by Islamic [law]. The conversion of the peoples of what are now the heartlands of the Islamic world was a largely peaceful process and was separate from the Arabs' military conquest of these same areas. Indeed, the [eventual] conversion [of many natives] largely resulted from the example set by the early Muslim Arabs themselves and the activities of preachers, missionaries, and merchants.[23]

Enter Uthman

Although a successful expansionist, Umar, like his predecessor, had his ambitious aims cut short while he was in his prime. In 644 a Persian prisoner of war broke free and attacked the caliph. According to a contemporary Arab chronicler,

When dawn came Umar went forth to prayer, and [when finished he] recited *Allahu akbar* ["God is great!"]. And [a slave named] Abu Lulu entered among the [worshippers], and in his hand was a dagger with two blades, and . . . he smote [hit] Umar six blows, one of them under the navel, and it was this one that killed him.[24]

Uthman ibn Affan, son-in-law of Muhammad, became the third caliph after Caliph Umar was assassinated.

God on Our Side?

One factor that inspired the members of various armies throughout history, from the ancient Israelis and Assyrians to early modern Europeans and Americans, was the belief that God was fighting on their side. Early Muslim soldiers felt the same way, and as noted American historian W.H. McNeill says here, that belief heavily contributed to their widespread success.

Surely the major determinant of Arab success was the discipline and courage inspired in the rank and file by the certainty, confirmed with each victory, that Allah was indeed fighting on their side. . . . The effort to remake human life according to the will of Allah . . . was equally significant in the cultural sphere. In its most extreme form, radical piety entailed suspicion of any activity not directly serving the ends of religion. Truth and beauty resided in the Quran. Any other repository [of knowledge and law], being merely human, distracted people from the pursuit of holiness.

W. H. McNeill. *The Rise of the West.* Chicago: University of Chicago Press, 1992, pp. 468, 475.

Almost with his last breath, Umar called for a committee of leading Arabs to select a new caliph from their own ranks. The choice was Uthman ibn Affan, a son-in-law of Muhammad. Overall, Uthman proved to be a capable and kindly ruler, although he was also an expansionist like his two predecessors. The Caliphate gained Libya (west of Egypt) under Uthman, as well as parts of Iran and Afghanistan (both lying east of Iraq). Uthman also created the first Muslim navy and seized the strategically located eastern Mediterranean island of Cyprus, which had been under Byzantine rule.

In spite of his many positive accomplishments, Uthman, like so many other rulers of large, diverse realms in history, found that he could not please all of his subjects all of the time. Some of his followers, for instance, complained they were being passed over for high government positions. The caliph was placing too many members of his own clan in those jobs, they said. When Uthman refused to deal with this grievance, in 656 a group of the protesters attacked his palace and assassinated him.

This mean-spirited and fateful act was destined to have colossal consequences. At the time, no one could foresee the enormous divisions and hatreds among Muslims that were about to be unleashed in the wake of Uthman's death. In the words of one modern expert, "Islam has been at war with itself ever since."[25]

Chapter Three

Islam Rocked by Civil Strife

In the aftermath of the murder of the third caliph, Uthman, most of the powerful energies that had carried Muslims outward to conquer neighboring peoples were suddenly directed inward. To the surprise and distress of all involved, the still young Islamic world was rocked by civil strife. The discord was caused by a number of disagreements within the Muslim community, the continuously growing *umma*.

But by far the main bone of contention was a sharp difference of opinion over how the community's leaders should be chosen. Some Muslims, who later came to be called the Shia (or Shiites), strongly felt that Muhammad's cousin and son-in-law, Ali, should succeed Uthman. Many others, who later became known as the Sunni, opposed this nomination. Paul Lunde, a specialist in Islamic history, explains the essentials of this argument, the most important in the history of the faith:

The supporters of Ali believed that he should have been the immediate successor of Muhammad, and that he had three times been unfairly passed over, [which led to] the schism of Islam into Sunni and Shia. . . . The Sunni, or "the people of custom and community," believe the caliph is Muhammad's successor only as ruler of the community, and that the caliph is [an] elective [position]. The Shia, or "partisans of Ali," believe the [office of caliph], which they call the imamate, is non-elective, and that the head of the Muslim community must be a [direct] descendant of Muhammad. They hold that the imam inherits the Prophet's spiritual knowledge and the ability to interpret Divine Law.[26]

These starkly contrasting beliefs provided the backdrop for a major confrontation and power struggle shortly after Uthman's passing. On one side was Ali himself. As a candidate for caliph, he enjoyed the support of a number of Muslims who hoped that having a descendent of the Prophet in power would make the community purer and closer to the faith's original precepts.

Opposing Ali was Uthman's cousin, Muawiya ibn Abi Sufian. Like Uthman, Muawiya was a member of the highly influential Umayyad clan. Also backing

Muhammad pledges his daughter to his cousin Ali. The rift in Islam occurred because Ali's backers, the Shia, believed that Muhammad's successor must be a direct descendant of the Prophet. Sunnis believed that Muhammad's successor was to be elected.

Muawiya were Muhammad's widow, Aisha, who strongly disliked Ali, and two of her own relatives, Talhah and Zubayr. The face-off between these two groups was of "the utmost importance in Islamic history," one modern expert points out, "because this is when the main sub-groups or sects that have constituted the Muslim community up to the present day first emerged."[27]

The Woman and the Camel

For a while, it appeared that Ali would easily overshadow his enemies and lead the *umma* for many years to come. Not long after Uthman's death in July 656, leading Muslims in Medina, who had Shia sympathies, recognized Ali as caliph. Wasting no time, the newly appointed ruler set up his capital at Kufa, in southern Iraq.

Meanwhile, Muawiya surprised very few when shortly afterward he announced he would not recognize Ali as caliph and would challenge him for that high office. Ali viewed Muawiya and his supporters as rebels against the community, much as Abu Bakr had seen the defiant bedouins in the wake of Muhammad's death in 632. The most logical course, the new caliph decided, was to seek out and neutralize the ringleader of the rebellion, Muawiya.

Before Ali could pursue this strategy, however, he found an obstacle in his path, namely the coalition of Aisha, Talhah, and Zubayr. The three had pieced together a small but formidable army (at first numbering about a thousand but later reinforced). They occupied Basra, situated southeast of Kufa. There, Aisha and her kinsmen seized the local governor as he was exiting a mosque. "The unfortunate man was humiliated with forty lashes," as one expert observer tells it, "after which the public executioner plucked out all his facial hair (including his eyebrows and eyelashes) before throwing him into prison."[28]

On hearing what had happened, Ali realized the rebels meant business. It was clear to him that their next move would be to launch a direct attack on his new capital. Determined to prevent what he viewed as a brazen assault on the *umma* itself, Ali mustered his own soldiers and marched on Basra. Arriving in early December 656, he attempted to talk Aisha and her compatriots out of continuing what he viewed as their traitorous behavior. It appears that he sincerely desired to find some way of avoiding bloodshed among members of the faith. But the negotiations eventually broke down, perhaps partly because of Aisha's stubbornness and burning hatred for Ali.

In the morning of December 8, the two armies clashed, formally inaugurating Islam's first civil war. During the fierce fighting, which lasted for several hours, Talhah and Zubayr were both slain. Soon after that, according to English scholar Barnaby Rogerson,

> the fighting concentrated around the camel litter [traveling platform] in which Aisha sat, protected by [leather] panels. Champion after champion from her ranks

The Twelvers and Their Beliefs

Like other Islamic groups, the Shia developed disagreements within their own ranks over time and split into different groups. Among the most influential of these groups is the Imamites, or "Twelvers," described by scholars Fred J. Hill and Nicholas Awde.

The Twelvers venerate twelve Imams in all, believing them to have been chosen by God and to be infallible. The final Imam was believed to have mysteriously disappeared in 873. From that time [on], the Twelvers began a long wait for his return as the "Mahdi," or "Messiah," and for the occasion when he would avenge the wrong-doings perpetrated against them by the more numerous Sunnis and restore justice in the prelude to the Last Judgment. Until the Twelfth Imam's return, it was the Shia's lot to suffer unjust rulers and their corrupt governments. To enable them to cope with the wider Muslim community, they practiced "taqiya," which permitted them in times of danger to conceal their true beliefs and melt into the mainstream and conform. The rebellion would wait until the coming of the Mahdi.

Fred J. Hill and Nicholas Awde. *A History of the Islamic World*. New York: Hippocrene, 2003, p. 35.

came forth to take the place of honor—and near certain death—by advancing to hold the camel halter [and] serve as her protective knight. One by one they were felled by [Ali's] surrounding archers. . . . It was said that forty young men [in some accounts seventy] took their death-pride in turn by guarding Aisha's camel before Ali gave the decisive order that the beast be hamstrung [crippled]. Ali gave orders that Aisha was to be escorted by her own young half-brother to a house in Basra, after which she was to be taken back to her home in Medina.[29]

With the battle at an end, the victorious caliph told his heralds to ride through the ranks of exhausted fighters and loudly proclaim: "No one turning his back shall be pursued. No one wounded shall be killed. Whoever throws away his arms is safe."[30] In a further display of leniency, Ali allowed his soldiers to take only weapons and animals as booty, based on his firm belief that no Muslims, even those who opposed him, should become slaves. In addition, he decreed that the dead on both sides be buried with due respect. Thereafter, because of the prominence of the camel in the fighting, the clash came to be called the Battle of the

Ali holds the body of the governor beaten almost to death by Aisha's supporters. At the subsequent Battle of the Camel, Ali's forces defeated Aisha's supporters.

Camel. (It is also sometimes referred to as the Battle of Basra because it took place near that city.)

Outrage over a Bloody Shirt

Over the centuries, historians have debated why Ali showed so much mercy to his opponents. Some have speculated that it was a political move intended to make him look like a fair, forgiving individual who would give all members of the *umma* a fair shake. That way, hopefully, many of those who had come to oppose him might have a change of heart and offer him their support. However, other expert observers have concluded that Ali's compassion and generosity were not feigned but rather actually part of his personality. As evidence, they point to the contents of the *Najh ul Balagha*, or *Way of Eloquence*, a surviving collection of letters and sayings attributed to Ali. In one of many reasonable and humane pieces of advice, he states,

Do not feel ashamed to forgive and forget. Do not hurry [to inflict] punishments and do not be . . . proud of your power to punish. Do not get angry and lose your temper quickly over the mistakes and failures of those over whom you rule. On the

The Sunnis' Views Explained

The eleventh-century Muslim writer al-Mawardi recorded the following justification for Sunni beliefs and rule.

The Imamate [ruler] is placed on earth to succeed the Prophet [i.e., Muhammad] in the duties of defending the Religion and governing the World, and it is religious obligation to give allegiance to that person who performs those duties. . . . He must be of the tribe of Quraysh [Muhammad's tribe], since there has come down an explicit statement on this, and the consensus [of most members of Islam] has agreed. . . . The Prophet said, "The Quraysh have precedence, so do not go before them," and there is no pretext for any disagreement, when we have this clear statement delivered to us, and no word that can raise against it.

Quoted in Marven Gettleman and Stuart Schaar, eds. *The Middle East and Islamic World Reader*. New York: Grove, 2003, p. 23.

contrary, be patient and sympathetic with them. Anger and desire [for] vengeance are not going to be of much help to you in your administration. Never say to yourself, "I am their Lord, their ruler, [and] I must be obeyed" . . . because such a thought will [make] you vain and arrogant [and] weaken your faith in religion. . . . If you ever feel any pride or vanity on account of your sway and rule over your subjects, then think of the supreme sway and rule of the Lord over the Universe . . . the supremacy of His Might and Glory, His Power to do things which you cannot even dream of doing, and His control over you which is more dominating than that which you can ever achieve over anything around you. Such thoughts will . . . reduce your arrogance and haughtiness and will take you back to the sanity which you had foolishly deserted.[31]

Seemingly trying to put such humbling advice into practice, Ali offered his chief rival, Muawiya, the chance for peace talks. But Muawiya had made up his mind that he, and not Ali, must be caliph. To justify his actions, Muawiya cited a verse from the Quran that states: "Whoever is slain unjustly, We have indeed given to his heir authority [to avenge him], so let him [the avenger] not exceed the just limits in slaying."[32] The way Muawiya described it, the person who needed avenging was the mild-mannered Uthman, who had been cruelly hacked to pieces by his dastardly assassins, who now backed Ali. To further stir up outrage, Muawiya had Uthman's blood-covered shirt carried from town to town and displayed in public. As a result, it soon became clear to the faithful on both sides that another battle for supremacy was inevitable.

This time the fighting took place at Siffin, on the banks of the Euphrates River in western Iraq. In late July 657, the opposing armies—each numbering in the tens of thousands (the exact troop strengths are unknown)—came to death grips. The desperate fighting lasted for three days and three nights, during which untold numbers of Muslims perished, yet the outcome remained undecided. Then, seemingly out of nowhere, a group of mounted warriors appeared and rode between the front ranks of the opposing armies. They had fastened open copies of the Quran to their lances. As the exhausted soldiers on both sides stopped and watched in bewilderment, the riders shouted, "The word of God! Let the word of God decide between us and you! Who will protect the border towns of Syria if [Muawiya's followers] are slain, and who will protect the people of Iraq after [Ali's followers] are gone? Let the book of God judge between you and us!"[33]

Exactly who these Quran-carrying men were is somewhat uncertain. The consensus of most historians is that the group consisted of members of one or both armies who felt it was wrong for Muslims to resort to bloodshed to settle their differences. Whoever they were,

The First Islamic Civil War

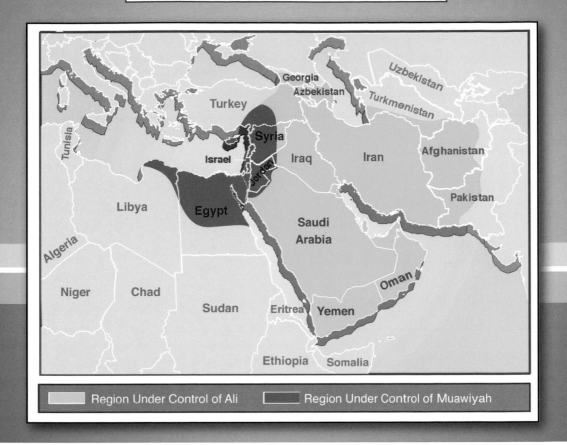

Region Under Control of Ali   Region Under Control of Muawiyah

their audacious performance succeeded in halting the battle. Ali and Muawiya agreed to a truce, during which a panel of respected Muslim elders would meet and choose between them for the position of caliph. The opposing commanders promised to abide by the decision of the panel, which would be handed down in the near future.

Two Caliphs?

While waiting for that fateful verdict, Ali encountered trouble from an unexpected quarter. As he led his weary soldiers back toward Kufa, about a third of them suddenly refused to make camp with him and the rest of the men. When asked why, they answered that they were mortified and angry over their leader's willingness to stop fighting, to compromise, and to allow unbiased parties to decide the future of the *umma* and its government.

Among the most conservative of Muslims at the time, these disgruntled men felt that both Ali and Muawiya had betrayed Muhammad's original beliefs and intentions. They demonstrated their anger and disgust by withdrawing, or seceding, from the *umma*. As a result, they came to be known as the Kharijites, meaning "seceders." (In the centuries that followed, the Kharijites stubbornly remained opposed to the caliphs, who in their view were not pious and spiritual enough. Today, calling themselves the Ibadi, they continue their tradition of separateness from the more numerous Sunni and Shia Muslims.)

The Kharijites not only refused to fight for Ali but also tried to undermine his power. When groups of these separatists began raiding the farms and villages of his followers, he felt he had no other choice but to quell their fanatical zeal. In May 658, near the site of modern Baghdad, he attacked and crushed them. Only a handful of the dissenters survived to pass on their purist beliefs to future generations.

In that same year, the panel of arbiters made its decision about who should be caliph. To the shock of all involved, the verdict was that both Ali and Muawiya should remove themselves from power and allow the members of the *umma* to elect a completely new leader. A good deal less shocking was the reaction of the two commanders. Going back on their promises, they immediately rejected the panel's judgment. Ali declared that he would remain caliph, while Muawiya soon announced that he too was caliph and had chosen Jerusalem as his capital.

The result was that for close to three years the Caliphate was divided into two vast sectors. The eastern one, ruled by Ali, stretched across Arabia, Iraq, Iran, and Afghanistan. The other, in the west, lorded over by Muawiya, included Syria, Palestine, Cyprus, and Egypt. Although the two sides remained technically at war, except for occasional small raids, each avoided battles and bloodshed. Apparently the mutual hope was that sooner or later their differences might be resolved peacefully.

Muawiya's Good Fortune

This stalemate was finally broken by an assassination plot. In 661 a group of the surviving Kharijites decided that if they could not overcome their enemies in battle, they would do so by stealth. The plan was to attack and kill both Muawiya and Ali and then place a Kharijite in power. Fortunately for Muawiya, one of his bodyguards caught a glimpse of the approaching assassin and tackled him, so the western caliph survived.

Ali was not so lucky, however. As he approached a group of petitioners (people asking the leader for favors), a killer named Ibn Muljam leaped forward and swung a broadsword at him. The caliph clung to life for two days before dying at sixty-three, the same age that his kinsman Muhammad had been when he passed away. Ali's sons feared that the Kharijites might desecrate their father's grave, so they buried him in a location that remains secret to this day.

Many of Ali's supporters hoped that his eldest son, Hasan, would succeed him as the eastern caliph and carry on the opposition to the western caliph, Muawiya. However, as University of Cambridge scholar Amira K. Bennison points out, Hasan was a practical man and when he saw that rule was beyond his grasp because he lacked sufficient support to fight Muawiya, he negotiated peace terms with him, including a substantial sum of money from the treasury of Kufa. In hindsight, the death of Ali marked the . . . start of a new era in which the [office of caliph] passed to [a series of] dynasties, whose political ethos [philosophy and approach to rule] blended the original [Arabian] idea of the Caliphate with various [Middle] Eastern traditions of kingship.[34]

An Umayyad mosque in Syria. Under the Umayyad dynasty the Islamic Empire was once again united, but the rift between Sunni and Shia remained.

The Farmer and the Chicken

Prolific British researcher and journalist Lesley Hazleton describes what happened when a small group of ultrapurist Kharijites who had condemned Ali for being too worldly tried to make an example of one of his close followers.

M atters came to a head when they chose the farmer son of an early companion of Muhammad's as their victim. [They] tied him up and dragged him together with his pregnant wife beneath [some] date palms. . . . They made the farmer kneel and watch as they disemboweled his wife, cut out the unborn infant, and ran it through with a sword. Then they cut off the farmer's head. . . . For Ali, the slaughter under the date palms was beyond contempt. He sent a message to [the killers, saying,] "As the Quran says, 'Indeed, this is clear depravity.' By God, if you had killed even a chicken in this manner, its killing would be a weighty matter with God. How will it be, then, with a human soul whose killing God has forbidden?"

Lesley Hazleton. *After the Prophet: The Epic Story of the Shia-Sunni Split in Islam.* New York: Doubleday, 2009, pp. 143–145.

This explains why the rule and royal courts of many of the dynastic caliphs that followed resembled those of the Persian, Greek, and Byzantine kings who had preceded the coming of Islam in the Middle East. Muawiya established the first of these dynasties, the Umayyad.

Strictly from a political standpoint, under the Umayyads the Islamic Empire was once more united. Religiously and philosophically, however, the *umma* was never again unified. This was because the division between Sunni and Shia endured (and remains in place today). In fact, the Shia refused to accept the legitimacy of Muawiya and the other Umayyad rulers. In the Shia view, only the imams, the heirs of Ali, were fit to rule all Muslims. Their justification for this belief was summarized by the noted medieval Muslim scholar al-Hilli, who said,

The Imam [must] be absolutely the best of the people of his age . . . [and] the Imam after the messenger of God [Muhammad] is Ali. And he is the best for two reasons. First, he is equal to the Prophet. And the Prophet is the best, hence his equal is also the best. Second, the Prophet had need of him, and of no one else of the companions and kindred [of Muhammad], in his prayer. And he who is needed is better than anyone else. . . . The word of the Prophet regarding him [was], "Ali is the best judge of you all." [Hence] it comes about that he [Ali] is the Imam [true leader of the faith].[35]

Because of their deep dislike for the Umayyads, the Shia remained a proverbial thorn in those rulers' sides. Expansion of the empire into foreign lands continued under the reigns of Muawiya's successors. But the caliphs were forced to constantly look inward as well as outward. A significant portion of their energies had to be devoted to keeping a sizable minority of their subjects from rising up and liquidating leaders whom the Shia viewed as usurpers and tyrants.

Chapter Four

A New Burst of Expansion

After gaining power over the entire Islamic empire, Muawiya and his chief supporters considered their position. They fully realized that the recent civil war had been fueled by friction between opposing claimants to the office of caliph. The problem was that ever since Muhammad's own passing, no stable policy for the succession had been established. As a solution to this dilemma, the new ruler and his backers chose to establish a family line of rulers—a dynasty. That way, when each caliph died, a son or other relative would take his place, and the transfer of power would be automatic and peaceful. During the eighty-nine years of the Umayyad dynasty that followed, that transfer of power occurred thirteen times. (Counting Muawiya, fourteen rulers in the Umayyad line oversaw the empire from 661 to 750.)

Muawiya and his immediate successors, who established their capital and power center in Damascus, Syria,

thought they were doing the best they could for their subjects. But later Muslim historians were mostly hostile to these leaders. The consensus of the critics was that the Umayyads accumulated a great deal of wealth, spent much of it on their own comforts, and worse, were not spiritual enough. Nevertheless, a few later Muslim scholars admitted that, despite their faults, the Umayyads did rack up a number of impressive achievements. Renowned expert on Islamic history Bernard Lewis, for instance, concedes that the Umayyads had faults but also gives them their due. In some ways, he says,

Muawiya and his descendants were a succession of remarkable rulers, seen as having maintained the stability and continuity of the Islamic state and society in a time of dangerous and disruptive internal struggles. The Umayyad caliphs accomplished this task through a series of compromises and interim [temporary] agreements which enabled them to preserve a measure of unity, to continue and extend the conquests [of neighboring lands], and to establish the nucleus of an imperial administration, society, and culture. [To their later discredit] they did this at the cost of some dilution of the pristine [pure] Islamic message. . . . Some Islamic precepts in such matters as administration and taxation were tacitly [quietly] set aside, and a system of government established . . . that relied more and more on the structure, [and] methods [of] the empires which the Islamic Caliphate had overthrown.[36]

The Umayyad dynasty made Damascus their center of power in the late seventh century.

The Umayyads' Early Troubles

Of course, most of the non-Arab, non-Muslim residents of the growing Islamic Empire were completely used to living under the autocratic systems that had long been traditional in the Middle East. So for them, the Umayyad rulers were no different than most of their predecessors. As for the Arabs dwelling throughout the realm, many were willing to accept Umayyad rule under certain conditions. First, their rights as Arab citizens and as Muslims free to practice their faith must be protected. Second, many Arabs wanted to see the empire continue expanding, as the zeal for conquest set in motion by Muhammad and the first three caliphs had not yet dissipated. For the most part, the Umayyad rulers met these conditions. They respected the basic rights of a majority of Arabs and Muslims and eventually greatly expanded the Islamic realm's borders. So for a long time most of their subjects gave them little or no trouble.

The minority who did cause difficulties for the dynasty early on were for the most part members of two groups—the Shia and Kharijites, both longtime opponents of various Muslim leaders. In 680, directly following Muawiya's death, the Shia once more stirred up unrest. A few years before, Muawiya had announced that he wanted his son Yazid to succeed him. The Shia had grumbled about the choice at the time, and now that Muawiya was gone, they stepped up their opposition to Yazid. Instead of choosing another Umayyad, they insisted, Mus-

---

The "Prince of Orators"

A quaint story has survived about the Umayyad caliph Muawiya's choice of his son Yazid to later follow him in that office:

The people gathered in the presence of Muawiya, and the orators rose to proclaim Yazid as heir to the Caliphate. Some of the people showed disapproval, whereupon a man in the tribe of Udhra . . . rose to his feet. Drawing his sword a handspan from the scabbard, he said, "The commander of the faithful is that one!" and pointed to Muawiya. "And if he dies, then that one!" and he pointed to Yazid. "And if anyone objects, then this one!" and he pointed to his sword. Muawiya said to him, "You are the prince of orators."

Quoted in Bernard Lewis, ed. and trans. *Islam, from the Prophet Muhammad to the Capture of Constantinople.* Vol. 2. New York: Oxford University Press, 1987, p. 273.

Painting of the battle of Karbala on October 10, 680. The army led by Yazid (center) defeated forces led by Husayn. The subsequent massacre of Husayn and his followers is a major commemorative event in the Shia calendar.

lims should elect Husayn (or Hussein), son of Ali and grandson of Muhammad, to the office of caliph. (This was squarely in line with the central Shia belief that only descendants of the Prophet should rule the Muslim community.)

Yazid and his followers remembered the hatreds and bloodshed of the civil war and wanted to try to avoid another devastating conflict among Muslims. If they rid themselves of young Husayn as swiftly as possible, they reasoned, the Shia cause would hopefully collapse. So Yazid ordered one of his military officers to take some soldiers and hunt down and kill Husayn. The latter fled with his family and some followers to the small settlement of Karbala, in central Iraq, where the soldiers caught up with them. On October 10, 680, the two

groups fought and Husayn and almost all of those with him were slain. According to Lewis,

Some seventy [of Husayn's party] were killed in the battle and its aftermath, the sole survivor being a sick child, Ali, the son of Husayn, who was left lying in a tent and lived to tell the story. The massacre of Karbala became central to the Shia perception of Islamic history, and the tenth day of Muharram [the first month in the Muslim calendar] became a major event [to the Shia]. Wherever Shia are to be found, on this day they commemorate the martyrdom of the Prophet's family, the penitence [remorse] of those who failed to save them, and the wickedness of those who killed them. . . . The massacre of Karbala speeded the transformation of the Shia from a political party to a religious sect.[37]

Thus, by resorting to violence in hopes of forestalling civil strife, Yazid and his supporters only succeeded in setting more conflict in motion. Indeed, a new round of hatred and bloodshed among Muslims erupted after Husayn's untimely end. On the one hand, some embittered and daring Kharijites attempted to set up their own Muslim states in Arabia. On the other, a rebellion led by Abdullah ibn Zubayr, the son of a veteran of the Battle of the Camel, began in 683. Only when a strong new Umayyad caliph, Abd al-Malik, came to power in 685 (after the deaths of Yazid and two short-lived successors) was the regime able to make some headway against the insurgents. By 692 all of al-Malik's adversaries had been eliminated, and peace and prosperity had been largely restored.

Arab Armies on the Move

While he was fighting and defeating his various opponents, al-Malik began initial planning for a new wave of Muslim conquests. He hoped these would begin soon after he had eliminated his internal enemies. While he was doing so, he took the opportunity to streamline and strengthen his imperial administration, which would make organizing his armies and any captured territories more efficient. To that end, he subdivided the government into departments, each run by a hand-picked bureaucrat. Al-Malik also made Arabic the empire's official language and issued the first Islamic coinage bearing Arabic words and symbols. These moves were designed to make Arab culture more ingrained in society throughout the realm.

In the early 690s, with his victories over ibn Zubayr and the other rebels complete, al-Malik finally mounted the military expeditions he had long been looking forward to. One army headed westward across coastal North Africa, a region the Arabs called the Maghreb. Another moved eastward and penetrated central Asia.

To lead the western campaigns the caliph chose a capable general named Hasan ibn al-Numan. Egypt and much of Libya were already in the Islamic fold, so ibn al-Numan set his sights on taking Carthage (in what is now Tunisia), then still a Byzantine stronghold. With some forty thousand soldiers, the biggest Muslim army fielded in the Maghreb up to that time, he was unstoppable. In 698 he defeated the Byzantines near Carthage and set up a naval base nearby to discourage them from trying to land more troops and retake the area. Carthage itself, which centuries before had been a thriving Roman town, was by now almost deserted, and most of the region's inhabitants lived in villages in the countryside. Ibn al-Numan chose one of these villages—Tunis—to become the Muslims' local base. This marked the start of its eventual growth into one of North Africa's most important cities.

Abd al-Malik (depicted on this coin) came to power in 685 and campaigned against his adversaries for seven years. After consolidating his power he made plans for further conquests.

Thereafter, Islamic expansion continued apace. In the west, following ibn al-Numan's death (sometime between 699 and 704), other Muslim commanders led troops to Africa's Atlantic coast. In the east, meanwhile, the caliph's soldiers overran territories lying northeast of Afghanistan, an area claimed by another famous conqueror, Alexander the Great, many centuries before.

One major reason for the remarkable success of Muslim armies like those of the caliph al-Malik and his generals was the attitude of their fighters. It consisted of a combination of self-confidence, personal and religious principle, and revolutionary zeal. Added to that singular overall outlook was the effectiveness of their traveling methods and battlefield tactics. Using mainly camels at first and later horses, when possible they moved along the edges of deserts, terrain they were familiar with, since so much of Arabia is made up of deserts. From such

Muslim armies used camels—and later horses—in their conquest of North Africa. The Muslim soldier, infused with religious zeal and self confidence, was a formidable opponent for opposing armies.

arid regions, which their enemies tended to avoid, they frequently launched surprise attacks on those enemies.

The Arab soldiers also often took along their women and children. The latter two groups took care of goats, sheep, and other livestock used to feed the army and tended to any wounded men. In addition, having their families along boosted the men's morale and fighting spirit, in part because they felt they must struggle all the harder in order to defend their loved ones. Some of the female camp followers occasionally grabbed hold of weapons and fought alongside their husbands, brothers, and fathers. This was somewhat uncommon. But at the least, when battle was imminent the women regularly whipped up their men to a fighting frenzy by beating drums and tambourines and reciting verses like the following surviving example: "On you sons of [great warriors], on [you] protectors of our rear [ranks], smite [strike] with every sharpened spear! If you advance, we hug you, [and] spread soft rugs beneath you. [But] if you retreat, we leave you, leave and no more love you!"[38]

As for the military tools and tactics employed by these spirited soldiers, once they had captured or bred enough horses they organized units of cavalry. These horsemen, armed with bows and large swords with razor-sharp blades, struck fast and hard at enemy armies, inflicting many casualties. Horses were very expensive to breed and maintain, however. So the primary battlefield units of the Arab armies were foot soldiers, or infantry, who wielded swords, knives, bows, spears, and iron maces (clubs), all of which they rigorously trained with beginning in their youth. A few fighters, mainly those who could afford it, wore mail (or chain-mail), a kind of armor consisting of many small iron rings interwoven to form a heavy, stiff, protective shirt. In contrast, a majority of fighters were able to afford shields. These were mostly round and made either of wood covered by animal hides or of metal, most often bronze (an alloy of copper and tin).

The Empire at Its Height

The new wave of Islamic expansion continued under al-Malik's successor, the Umayyad caliph Al-Walid. In the east in 712, a Muslim army reached the Indus River, in ancient times viewed as the gateway to India, and seized parts of the fertile Indian region known as the Punjab. Meanwhile, far to the north, a second Muslim army fought its way through the region of Transoxania and reached the western boundaries of China. Almost simultaneously, in the west in 711 contingents of a third Muslim army departed North Africa and crossed the Strait of Gibraltar into southern Spain. There, they routed a force of Visigoths (a tribal Christian people) that had gathered in hopes of halting the invasion. According

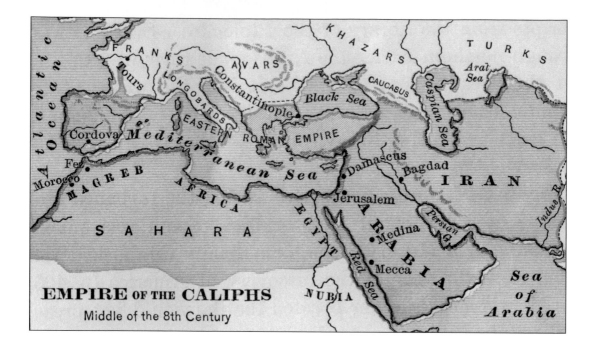

EMPIRE OF THE CALIPHS

Middle of the 8th Century

to later Muslim historians, news of all three armies' successes reached the caliph in Damascus on the same day (although many modern scholars find this difficult to believe).

By 713 all of Spain except the areas in the far north was in Muslim hands, and the Islamic Empire had reached its greatest geographical extent. It covered a bit more than 5 million square miles (13 million sq. km), making it the seventh-largest empire in world history. The Caliphate also encompassed about 62 million people, approximately 30 percent of the global population at the time.

Yet the Umayyad rulers apparently felt that this already enormous realm was still not large enough. In 718, when the caliph Umar II was in power, Muslim raiding parties crossed over the Pyrenees Mountains in northern Spain and entered the region inhabited by a

European people called the Franks. Then known as Francia, centuries later it would go by the more familiar name of France. The raiders captured the town of Narbonne, on the Mediterranean coast, and proceeded northward a little at a time. By 725 they had sacked Lyon, Vienne, and Autun, the latter located just 200 miles (322 km) southeast of Paris. Fearing the intruders would eventually absorb all of France and move deeper into Europe, several armies made up of Franks and other peoples of Germanic stock struck back. However, these attempts to stop the Muslim advance were only marginally successful.

The largest Muslim assault on France occurred in 732. The Umayyad caliph Hisham (reigned 724–743) allowed Abdul Rahman al Ghafiqi, then the governor of Muslim-controlled Spain, to lead a large army into Frankish territory.

This time the Franks and their German allies rallied behind a tough and talented war leader named Charles Martel. In 732 Martel and his men moved to stop al Ghafiqi and his equally determined followers near Tours, in west-central France.

As the two armies approached each other, Martel ordered his soldiers to come together in a tightly packed rectangular formation. This was likely designed to counter the deadly charge of the Muslim horsemen, who had earned a deserved reputation for fierceness in the prior decade. Sure enough, al Ghafiqi's cavalry made several frontal attacks on the Frankish defensive formation. But to the Muslim commander's surprise, the opposing ranks held their ground and repulsed each attack. A surviving Muslim chronicle provides a bit more detail of the Battle of Tours (or Poitiers), saying,

The Muslim horsemen dashed fiercely and frequently forward against the battalions of the Franks, who resisted manfully, and many fell dead on either side, until the going-down of the sun. . . . Many of the Muslims were fearful for the safety of the spoil [booty recently taken from captured towns] which they had stored in their tents, [and] several squadrons of the Muslim horsemen rode off to protect their tents. . . . And while [al Ghafiqi] strove to [stop them] and lead them

Battling for Political Rivalry

As medieval warfare expert David Nicolle explains, at the time it was fought, in 732, the battle of Tours (or Poitiers) was not viewed as a major confrontation between Islam and Christianity, as it is often portrayed today.

The clash between the Franks and Umayyads was less an ideological clash between Christianity and Islam, but resulted more from political rivalry and the desire to dominate a wealthy territory. [In whatever way] the battle [came to be seen] in the eyes of later historians, at the time it was just one event in a period of complex confrontations, during which rulers or governors were as likely to form alliances with those across the religious frontier as they were with those who shared their religion. This was certainly not a period when anyone other than a few church leaders saw events as a major confrontation between Islam and Christianity.

David Nicolle. *The Great Islamic Conquests, A.D. 632–750.* Oxford: Osprey, 2009, p. 73.

back to battle, the warriors of the Franks came round him and he was pierced through with many spears, so that he died. Then all the [Muslim] host fled before the enemy, and many died in the flight.[39]

Martel's forces had not only won the day, but also ground the powerful Muslim military thrust to a permanent halt.

The surviving invaders made their way back to Spain, where their families and friends were astounded that they had been beaten so badly. So damaging was their defeat that Spain's Muslim leaders were never again able to regain the momentum needed to capture any more of Europe. (Some modern European historians claim that Martel "saved" all of Europe from Muslim domination. How-

Charles Martel's victory over al Ghafiqi's Muslim horsemen at the battle of Tours in 732 reversed the tide of Muslim conquest in Europe.

The Dome of the Rock

Although the Umayyads were enthusiastic military expansionists, they also cared about domestic issues, including the arts. In fact, their artisans created the first examples of significant Islamic architecture, including the magnificent Dome of the Rock, described here by the acclaimed scholar of Islam Albert Hourani.

In the 690s, there was erected the first great building which clearly asserted that Islam was distinct and would endure. This was the Dome of the Rock, built on the site of the Jewish Temple in Jerusalem. . . . It was to be an ambulatory [a place for strolling and meditation] for pilgrims around the rock where, according to [tradition], God had called upon Abraham to sacrifice [his son] Isaac. The building of the Dome in this place has been convincingly interpreted [by experts] as a symbolic act placing Islam in the lineage of Abraham and dissociating [separating] it from Judaism and Christianity. The inscriptions around the interior, the earliest known physical embodiment of texts from the Quran, proclaim the greatness of God, "the Mighty, the Wise," declare that "God and his angels bless the Prophet [Muhammad]," and call upon Christians to recognize Jesus as an apostle of God, his word, and spirit, but not his son.

Albert Hourani. *A History of the Arab Peoples.* New York: Grand Central, 1991, p. 28.

The Dome of the Rock shrine on Temple Mount in Jerusalem is one of the finest examples of Umayyad dynasty architecture.

ever, no evidence exists that al-Ghafiqi and other Muslim commanders intended to venture beyond France.)

Corruption and Collapse

To their credit, the Umayyad rulers had pushed the borders of the Islamic empire outward to what seemed to them almost the ends of the earth. But they were unable to effectively rule or even hold together this vast realm for very long. Simply to administer so many lands and peoples, many of them lying thousands of miles from the capital, was difficult enough. Another problem was the great diversity of the conquered peoples. Most were non-Arab. Yet some of them had converted to Islam of their own accord, comprising a fast-growing group that came to be called the *mawali.*

Most of these recent converts felt that Arab Muslims held too much social prestige and political power at the expense of non-Arab Muslims. When most of the Umayyad caliphs made no effort to deal with this grievance, groups of *mawali* launched insurrections, which increased in number over the years. One of the worst took place in 739 in North Africa. A contingent of *mawali* known as the Berbers held out for three years against thousands of the caliph's troops before suffering defeat.

The caliph Umar II was the only Umayyad ruler with the good sense to try to introduce major reforms. He wanted to give non-Arab citizens of the empire social equality with Arabs. However, Umar died (in 720) before he could properly institute such improvements, and none of his mostly inept or corrupt successors followed up on his efforts. As a result, anti-Umayyad forces, including *mawali*, Kharijites, and Shia, grew increasingly stronger. One group of rebellious Shia wanted to replace the existing dynasty with caliphs descended from Abbas, one of Muhammad's uncles. Identifying themselves directly with Abbas, they took the name "Abbasids."

In 750 the Abbasids soundly defeated the last Umayyad caliph, Marwan II, and when he fled to Egypt, his administration and dynasty collapsed. A new era had dawned on the huge Islamic Empire. Exactly what the new dynasty would be like was a mystery to the realm's millions of residents. Only later would they discover the strange paradox (contradiction) of Abbasid rule. In an unexpected turn of events, some of the worst tyrants known to history would preside over the greatest cultural golden age Islam would ever know.

Chapter Five

Baghdad and Its Challengers

The medieval Islamic Empire reached its largest geographical size under the Umayyad dynasty. When that line of rulers ended in 750, many of the inhabitants of the realm wondered if the new line of caliphs—the Abbasids—would continue the policy of expansion that had begun with the Prophet himself in the early 600s. Would the empire continue to grow and perhaps eventually encompass the entire known world?

The passage of time soon provided an answer to such speculation. Almost from the beginning, the Abbasids demonstrated that they had little interest in further conquests. In fact, although they initially engaged in a few minor military campaigns, the focus of their rule was mainly inward. They were extremely preoccupied with maintaining their own power, authority, prestige, and comforts and delegated the running of the empire on a daily basis to underlings.

As a result of this insular attitude, politically speaking, the vast realm carved out in the previous century-and-a-half stagnated and lay open to power grabs by ambitious Muslim individuals and dynasties. The Abbasids did have impressive staying power. Indeed, their dynasty lasted for more than five centuries. However, during those centuries their empire shrank as, little by little, rival Muslims stripped away large chunks of territory. Thus, when a terrifying non-Muslim enemy eventually appeared on the eastern horizon, no large, united Islamic state was left to resist it, and millions of Muslims paid a heavy price.

A Fascination for Old Persia

In hindsight, one major reason the Islamic Empire decreased in size and power under the Abbasids was their approach to rule. As much as the Umayyads had been criticized for not being spiritual enough, they at least had done their best to rule as earlier Arab leaders had. In contrast, the thirty-seven Abbasid caliphs abandoned many Islamic political and governmental customs. Instead, they ruled more like the absolute monarchs of ancient Persia and the Byzantine Empire. No longer was the caliph seen as spiritually and morally equal to (though obviously more powerful than) other Muslim men. The Abbasids saw themselves as spiritually better than others—indeed as Allah's "shadows," or enforcers, on earth. Allowing power to go to their heads, some of them became cold-hearted tyrants. "Court ceremonies followed suit," historian Judith M. Bennett writes. The new palace rituals emphasized

> the awesome power of the caliphs in ways reminiscent of other [past] Eastern empires. Persian and Byzantine customs also began to affect gender roles, as the Abbasids adopted a variety of customs— such as the seclusion of women in private quarters, and the covering of women behind veils and draperies—which had not [earlier] been a general part of Islamic practice.[40]

The Abbasids' fascination for old Persia and Mesopotamia was also reflected in their decision to move the imperial capital from Damascus to Baghdad, in south-central Iraq, in 763. One modern historian describes Abbasid Baghdad, which rapidly grew into a grand metropolis on the banks of the Tigris River:

> The name of the city [is] Persian and means "Gift of God." It comes from the name of a small village that stood on the site of the new city. Al-Mansur, the [Abbasid] caliph who founded the city, chose the site because of the good air and the fact that the Tigris was a major commercial artery, linking the city to the [Persian] Gulf and ultimately to the sea route to China, already opened by Muslim traders. . . . The core of the city, housing the caliph, his administrators, slaves, and personal guard, was laid out according to cosmological principles, probably of Persian origin. It was circular, with concentric [walls] marking off the different quarters. In the center was the caliph's palace. . . . Beyond the outer wall of [that concealed abode], suburbs grew up, and Baghdad shortly became one of the largest cities in the world.[41]

The reference to walls surrounding the Abbasids' central palace, hidden from view of their subjects, is telling. These rulers lived almost like hermits and only rarely made public appearances. According to Amira K. Bennison,

> The caliphs disappeared from public view and only emerged in full ceremonial regalia [formal outfits] shaded by [a large umbrella-like apparatus], previously a Persian symbol of kingship. They received petitions and visitors via their ministers and chamberlains, whose power

was thus [aided] by their ability to control access to the caliphal presence. . . . If the stories [of] the time are to be believed . . . the caliphs and their close male relatives escaped the sometimes [suffocating] life of their palaces in Baghdad by [roaming] the streets in disguise to find out what was happening [among the people].[42]

Although the Abbasids' approach to rule was highly autocratic and intended to create an aura of secrecy and fear among their subjects, the empire was initially stable and peaceful. In large

The Abbasids built Kadiomin Mosque in Baghdad. The Abbasids' fascination with old Persia and Mesopotamia was reflected in their decision to move their imperial capital from Damascus to Baghdad.

The Thriving Abbasid Economy

University of Chicago scholar Fred M. Donner here provides a brief snapshot of the enormous economic dimensions of the Abbasid realm.

Hoards of Abbasid gold coins found around the Baltic Sea [north of Poland] are silent reminders of a once-thriving commercial connection that helped revitalize the economy of northern Europe. . . . The discovery of North African coins in Abbasid-period archaeological sites in Jordan, or Iraqi (or Chinese) ceramics found in Egypt, attest to yet other dimensions of this thriving commerce. It is appropriate to think of much of Eurasia in this period as a single, vast economic body, of which Abbasid Baghdad in particular was the heart, pumping the commercial lifeblood that kept the system alive. Iraq's prosperity in particular, with its rich tax base and thriving commerce, was an important element contributing to the political power and cultural brilliance of the high caliphate. When Iraq's agrarian prosperity began to wane in the tenth century . . . the caliphs found themselves increasingly unable to pay the bills of their enormous government operations.

Fred M. Donner. "Muhammad and the Caliphate." In *The Oxford History of Islam*, edited by John L. Esposito. New York: Oxford University Press, 1999, p. 32.

This imitation gold dinar, found in England, a copy of the dinars struck by the Abbasids, has an Arabic inscription on one side and was probably used in trade. It attests to the economic influence of the Abbasid dynasty.

part this was because its economy was strong, which made for decent living standards for many people. The financial powerhouse that drove much of the economy was Baghdad itself. It became an always busy and immensely successful trading hub for exporting and importing a wide array of goods from North Africa and Spain in the west and India and China in the east.

Traders from Baghdad and other Abbasid cities also ventured to the south of Egypt (into the region called Nubia in ancient and medieval times) and then southwestward into north-central Africa. In this way, new trade routes were forged with the prosperous kingdoms lying south of the Sahara Desert. Based on their long-standing contacts with Muslim merchants, many of the residents of these states eventually converted to Islam.

Rise of the Fatimids

Partly because of the wealth generated by merchants and bankers in the thriving Abbasid cities, over time the dynasty in Baghdad began to face serious challenges from other Muslim groups and dynasties. One of the strongest and most motivated at first was the Fatimids, who ruled Egypt and parts of North Africa from 909 to 1171. The Fatimids had their origins in Shia Islam, which remained as potent a minority within the Abbasid realm as it had been under the Umayyads. Throughout both dynasties, the Shia continued to hold dear a succession of imams, whom they viewed as the descendants of Muhammad and his cousin Ali.

In 765 the sixth imam, Jafar al-Dasiq, passed away, and most Shia recognized his son Musa as the next imam. However, a few Shia believed that another of Dasiq's sons, Ismail, was the true seventh imam, so they became known as the Ismailis as well as the "Seveners." The Ismailis managed to establish a small power base in Yemen, in the southwestern sector of the Arabian Peninsula. From there, they sent agents to Tunisia, in North Africa, where they found many sympathizers among the locals. Soon the Tunisian Ismailis had their own army, and in about 909 they started their own dynasty, the Fatimids, named for Fatima, Muhammad's daughter and Ali's wife.

The Fatimids openly defied the Abbasid caliphs, still entrenched in Baghdad. "For the first time," Bernard Lewis points out, "a powerful independent dynasty ruled" within the Islamic Empire, one "that did not recognize [the] authority of the Abbasids, but on the contrary founded a caliphate of their own, challenging the Abbasids for the headship of the whole Islamic world."[43]

Part of this challenge was military. In 969 the fourth Fatimid caliph, al-Muizz, sent an army of some one hundred thousand men to conquer Egypt. When this was accomplished, work began on a new capital—Qahira, now known as Cairo. Another aspect of the Fatimids' challenge was economic. Once they had control of Egypt, they lured a great deal of Asian trade away from the Persian Gulf and to the Red Sea, which hurt the Abbasids in their pocketbooks.

This Fatimid-minted coin is illustrative of the theological split with the Abbasids. The design of concentric circles has inscriptions referring to the Fatimids' Shia beliefs rather than the usual Abbasid inscriptions.

The Seljuks and Crusades

One reason the caliphs in Cairo did not become strong enough to topple the Abbasids was that the Fatimids eventually had to deal with a powerful challenge of their own. This competition came from the Seljuks (or Saljuqs), who created an enormous empire stretching across Anatolia, parts of the Middle East, and western Asia from 1037 to 1194. (Those Seljuks who entered Anatolia became the ancestors of the Turks.) The Seljuks were a Muslim group native to the region north of the Caspian Sea, in south-central Asia. When they felt they were strong enough, they pushed westward and in the 1050s seized Iraq, including Baghdad. They did not overthrow the Abbasids, however. Instead, perhaps out of respect for Islamic tradition, they allowed the Abbasid caliphs to

remain in power as long as they did the Seljuk's bidding in international affairs and did not interfere with major Seljuk affairs and goals.

The Seljuks not only seized large parts of the Islamic Empire from the Abbasids but also helped to provoke a long series of wars known as the Crusades. In 1071 the Seljuks captured Palestine, including Jerusalem. That area was viewed as the "Holy Land" by most Europeans, who were Christians, because it was where Jesus and his initial followers had lived and died. The Abbasids and other Muslims who had earlier ruled Jerusalem had not bothered the thousands of Christian pilgrims who visited the city each year. The Seljuks, however, levied a tax on and otherwise interfered with the pilgrims.

In Italy, Pope Urban II heard what had happened and became determined to help the Christian travelers by ridding Palestine of all Muslims. (He did not distinguish among Abbasids, Seljuks, Fatimids, and so forth; to him, they were all heathens, or non-Christians, and therefore a less civilized people.) In 1095 Urban called upon the Christian nobles of Europe to go to war and cleanse the Holy Land of heathens. He stated in part that God wanted "knights and foot-soldiers, rich and poor, to hasten to exterminate this vile race from the [Holy Land], and to bear timely aid to the worshippers of Christ." It was an utter disgrace, he added, that "a race so despised [and] degenerate" had taken control of the Holy Land.[44]

The pope's words set in motion the First Crusade, which lasted from 1095 to 1099. Tens of thousands of Europeans of all walks of life journeyed eastward to fight the "Saracens," which was then the general European term for any and all Muslims. Various contingents of crusaders were led by kings, dukes, priests, and general rabble-rousers. Nearly all were filled with genuine religious fervor, believing their faith was the only true one and had to be defended to the death. It was this zeal, not unlike that

This medieval illuminated manuscript depicts Pope Urban II at the 1095 Council of Clermont. He called for a holy war, or Crusade, to take back Palestine from the Muslims.

which at times had motivated Muslim armies, that led to the capture of Jerusalem in July 1099. One of the crusaders, a Frenchman named Fulk of Chartres, later described some of the carnage that followed:

> On Friday [July 15, 1099], with trumpets sounding, [and] amid great commotion and shouting, "God help us," the [French] entered the city. [The Saracens] were completely demoralized, and [some of them] took refuge in . . . the Temple of Solomon. . . . In this temple almost ten thousand [Saracens] were killed. Indeed, if you had been there, you would have seen our feet colored to our ankles with the blood of the slain. . . . None of them were left alive. Neither women nor children were spared.[45]

Saladin and the Ayyubids

After taking Jerusalem, the crusaders established several small Christian kingdoms in the region. Together, they came to be called the Outremer, or "lands overseas." But the Christians were unable to maintain control of Jerusalem and its environs. These were recaptured in 1187 by a Muslim army commanded by one of the finest generals and statesmen ever produced by medieval Islam. His name was Saladin.

Saladin achieved fame and substantial power by capturing sizable tracts of territory from both the Fatimids and Seljuks. Brought up in Seljuk-controlled Syria, he became a high-ranking commander under Nur ad-Din, the governor of the Seljuk Syrian province. In 1169 Saladin led a small army to Egypt, where a force commanded by the Christian king of Jerusalem was besieging the Fatimid capital of Cairo. The Christians fled at Saladin's approach. Then, out of gratitude, the Fatimid caliph, Al-Adid, gave him the title of Prince Defender.

Al-Adid turned out to be the last of the Fatimids, because shortly after he died in 1171, Saladin seized power in Egypt. He proceeded to establish his own Muslim dynasty—the Ayyubids (a term derived from Saladin's family name, Ayyub). Because he was Sunni Muslim, Saladin restored Sunni rule to Egypt after more than two centuries of control by the Shia Fatimids. He then wasted no time in turning on his Seljuk benefactors and conquering large sectors of their empire. During these campaigns, Saladin, like the Seljuks before him, left the Abbasid caliphs in place in Baghdad, where they steadily began to regain some of their former authority and influence.

In addition to his naked ambition, boldness, and military prowess, Saladin became known for his chivalry and hospitality, which sometimes extended even to his enemies. For example, when England's king, Richard I (the so-called

This fourteenth-century illuminated manuscript depicts the crusaders' capture of Jerusalem and the subsequent massacre of the population in 1099.

The Kurdish-born Saladin conquered territories of the Seljuks and the Fatimids and seized power after the last Fatimid ruler died. He recaptured Jerusalem in 1187.

"Lionheart"), was wounded in battle during the Third Crusade, Saladin offered him the service of his personal physician. This humane approach to warfare became that Muslim leader's trademark. Efraim Karsh explains:

Reflecting neither a burning spirit of jihad, nor an unwavering anti-Christian enmity [hatred], this [chivalrous] behavior epitomized Saladin's career. . . . [His] attitude toward the [Abbasid and European crusader] states was above all derived from his lifelong effort at empire-building. As long as they did not stand in the way of his endeavors, he was amenable to leaving them in peace or even to maintaining mutually benefi-

Rituals of Murder and Suicide

The Assassins murdered not only Muslim leaders but also a few Christian ones during the Crusades. A Christian writer of the period, Arnold of Lubeck, wrote that the leader of the Assassins in Syria, the so-called Old Man of the Mountain, helped some of his followers commit suicide after they had carried out their gory assignments.

By his witchcraft, [the Old Man] so bemused [bewildered] the men of his country [i.e., Syria], that they neither worship nor believe in any god but himself. Likewise he entices them in a strange manner with such hopes and with promises of such pleasures with eternal enjoyment, that they prefer rather to die than to live. Many of them, when standing on a high wall, will jump off at his nod or command, and shattering their skulls, die a miserable death. The most blessed, so he affirms, are those who shed the blood of men and in revenge for such deeds themselves suffer death. When therefore any of them have chosen to die in this way . . . he himself hands them knives [and] promises them eternal possession of [pleasures and delights] in reward for such deeds.

Quoted in Bernard Lewis. *The Assassins.* New York: Basic Books, 2003, p. 4.

The Assassins' castle at Masyaf in Syria. From fortresses like this one, the Assassins infiltrated city crowds and other groups to reach their targets.

cial economic and political relationships with them. But when a unique opportunity to land a shattering blow presented itself, he had no qualms about seizing the moment, just as he unhesitatingly ended hostilities when such action had outlived its usefulness. There was nothing personal about this behavior. It was strictly business.[46]

New and Dangerous Enemies

In spite of his political shrewdness, Saladin did not foresee the degree to which state affairs and the power balance in the Middle East was about to change. Partly because of his own conquests, the once dominant Seljuk dynasty ended in 1192. Saladin himself passed away the following year, and much of the region broke up into smaller Muslim kingdoms. Their leaders continued to resist European invaders who kept initiating new Crusades designed to recapture the Holy Land. These campaigns all failed. In the meantime, moreover, the Muslims assaulted the small states of the European Outremer, all of which were erased from the map by the late 1200s.

Although the European threat to Palestine and surrounding lands was gone, another, no less dangerous enemy remained. The surviving Abbasid caliphs and other Muslim leaders in the Middle East encountered a long-term threat from within their own midst. It took the form of a group of rebel terrorists known as the Assassins (from whose name the English word *assassin* derives). An extreme offshoot of the Shia Ismailis, they concluded that most Muslim rulers were far too worldly and corrupt and therefore must be removed from power by any means necessary. Most often that means was murder.

The Assassins began killing caliphs and other leaders, mostly in Syria, Iraq, and Iran, in the late eleventh century. Descending from their remote, inaccessible mountain fortresses, they skillfully infiltrated city crowds and other groups in order to reach their high-status targets. According to Lewis, who wrote the definitive book on the Assassins,

> Their weapon was almost always the same—the dagger, wielded by the appointed Assassin in person. . . . Having struck down the assigned victim, [the killer] made no attempt to escape, nor was any attempt made to rescue him. On the contrary, to have survived a mission was seen as a disgrace.[47]

Although the Assassins managed to slay several caliphs, they were unable to eradicate the Abbasid realm or neighboring Islamic states. The force that did eventually destroy most of the eastern remnants of the formerly immense Islamic Empire came from outside the Muslim world. In the 1240s and 1250s an extremely aggressive people known as the Mongols suddenly swept out of east-central Asia. They rapidly overran Iran and Iraq, sacked Baghdad, and executed the last Abbasid ruler and his fam-

Baghdad Becomes a Ruin

The Mongols sacked and burned the magnificent metropolis of Baghdad and killed most of its residents. According to the fourteenth-century Muslim historian Ibn Kathir,

The Mongols surrounded the seat of the Caliphate and rained arrows on it from every side until a slave girl was hit while she was . . . dancing before the caliph. [He] was alarmed and very frightened. [After he met with the Mongol leader, who refused to make peace, the Mongols] came down upon the city and killed all they could, [including] men, women, and children, the old, the middle-aged, and the young. Many of the people went into wells, latrines, and sewers and hid there for many days without emerging. . . . [The invaders] killed them . . . until blood poured from the gutters into the street. . . . The same happened in the mosques [and] convents. [And so] Baghdad, which had been the most civilized of all cities, became a ruin with only a few inhabitants, and they were in fear and hunger and wretchedness and insignificance.

Quoted in Bernard Lewis, ed. and trans. *Islam, from the Prophet Muhammad to the Capture of Constantinople.* Vol. 1. New York: Oxford University Press, 1987, pp. 83–84.

ily. The leader of the invaders, Hulegu Khan, gave the following rationale for invading the Muslim lands:

God the eternal elevated Genghis Khan [the founder of the Mongol Empire] and his progeny [offspring] and gave us [everything on] the face of the earth, from east to west. Anyone whose heart and tongue are straight with us in submission retains his kingdom, property, women, children, and life. . . . He who contemplates otherwise will not live to enjoy them.[48]

A number of Muslim states, including those in western Arabia, North Africa, and Spain, survived the Mongol incursion. Also, Iraq and other eastern regions devastated by the invaders eventually recovered and became incorporated into new Muslim nation-states. A few of these states survived into modern times and became economically successful and culturally vibrant countries. But strictly from a territorial standpoint, none ever came close in size and imperial majesty to the medieval Islamic Caliphate at its height in the mid-700s. By that standard, Alfred Guillaume says, in late medieval times Muslim civilization "suffered a blow from which it has never entirely recovered."[49]

Chapter Six

Islamic Culture's Golden Age

Although the Mongol invasions and fall of the Abbasid dynasty marked the end of the once vast medieval Islamic Caliphate, some aspects of that historic empire in a very real sense lived on. In particular, the Abbasid centuries, especially the first three (ca. 750–1050), produced one of history's most splendid cultural golden ages. In many ways it was similar, as well as equal in scope and quality, to the Periclean Age in fifth-century B.C. Athens and the European Renaissance in the fourteenth and fifteenth centuries A.D. All three generated numerous superb examples of art, architecture, literature, and science.

Many people in the modern West know only about their own great ancestral ages of achievement in Greece, Rome, and Renaissance Europe. They do not realize that when Islam's golden age was in full sway, European culture as a whole was considerably more back-

ward. Indeed, in early medieval times Europeans were far behind their Muslim counterparts in science and the arts. It is also interesting to note that Muslim intellectuals of that age knew they were ahead of the West and often viewed Europeans with contempt. The tenth-century Muslim geographer al-Masudi said of the latter, "Their natures [are] gross, their manners harsh, their understanding dull, and their tongues heavy. . . . The farther they live to the north, the more they are stupid, gross, and brutish."[50]

Travel, Education, and Translation

Several varied factors came together to produce Islam's great cultural outburst, which was centered in Abbasid Baghdad. First, the wide-ranging trade carried on by that city and others across the Islamic Empire took Muslim merchants to many distant lands. Diplomats and

76 ■ The Islamic Empire

other individuals from Baghdad also traveled far and wide. Among the better known was Ahmad ibn Fadlan, who in 922 journeyed to what is now Russia and studied its people and their customs. These travelers' exposure to other cultures and their ideas helped to widen the creative horizons of Muslim thinkers, artisans, and educators.

In turn, education in both the Umayyad and Abbasid caliphates became more widespread than in earlier Arabic cultures. Many Muslim men could read at a time when the vast majority of Europeans were illiterate. Moreover, among the Muslims who became well educated, several went further and pushed the boundaries of learning, especially in the areas of literature, philosophy, and science. Al-Kindi, a philosopher active in the early 800s, summed up an attitude that had by then become common among Muslim thinkers. "We should not be ashamed to acknowledge truth from whatever source it comes to us," he said, "even if it is brought to us by former generations and foreign peoples. For him who seeks the truth, there is nothing of higher value than truth itself."[51]

No less crucial to the expansion of Islamic philosophy and science in the Abbasid age was the rediscovery and translation of numerous ancient Greek literary works that had been lost to Europe after western Rome's fall. The caliph al-Mamun, who came to power

This woodcut depicts Caliph al-Mamun with his astronomers. Al-Mamun ordered translations of works by large numbers of ancient Greek authors and founded the Academy of Wisdom in Baghdad.

in 813, ordered large numbers of Greek, Persian, and Indian books to be translated into Arabic. That caliph also established Baghdad's Academy of Wisdom, where thinkers and scholars compiled huge amounts of knowledge from many lands. As a result of this intellectual activity, Muslim scholars began turning out explanations, commentaries, and critiques of the works of Aristotle and other ancient thinkers. Some of the Muslim thinkers who read these analyses then went on to produce their own original works in several literary and scientific disciplines.

Mathematics, Geography, and Astronomy

In fact, the strides that educated Muslims made in science were among the most extraordinary accomplishments of the golden age. In the words of Georgetown University professor Ahmad Dallal,

> Science was practiced on a scale unprecedented in earlier or contemporary human history. In urban centers from the Atlantic to the borders of China, thousands of [Muslim] scientists pursued careers in diverse scientific disciplines. . . . Their written contributions are equally compelling. Thousands of scientific manuscripts from various regions of the medieval Islamic world are scattered in modern libraries all over the globe. . . . Until the rise of modern science, no other civilization engaged as many scien-

tists, produced as many scientific books, or provided as varied and sustained support for scientific activity.[52]

One of the most profound and enduring examples of this activity was the Muslim math whiz al-Khwarizmi's introduction of so-called Arabic numerals. Fascinated by Indian mathematics, he based his numerals on an ancient Hindu number system. Researcher Michael H. Morgan explains that it was "a decimal system with characters representing quantities ranging from 0 to 9, and then arranged in combination to reach up and down into positive and negative infinity from the source dot of zero," or the now familiar decimal point. Al-Khwarizmi and his colleagues saw that this system, today the most common one in use across the world, met a wide range of mathematical needs, including "calculating the area of irregular spaces; finding missing quantities using the relationship of known ones; [and] calculating the relationship of the Earth to the sun and stars."[53]

Indeed, Arabic numerals were so simple and easy to use that they made mathematical calculation much easier than it had been in the past. Al-Khwarizmi's system started to filter into Europe beginning in the late 900s. In the centuries that followed, they made work and life easier for scientists and ordinary people alike throughout the Western lands and across the globe. "The Hindu-Arab numbers," Morgan continues, became "essential" to later science. "Modern technology and

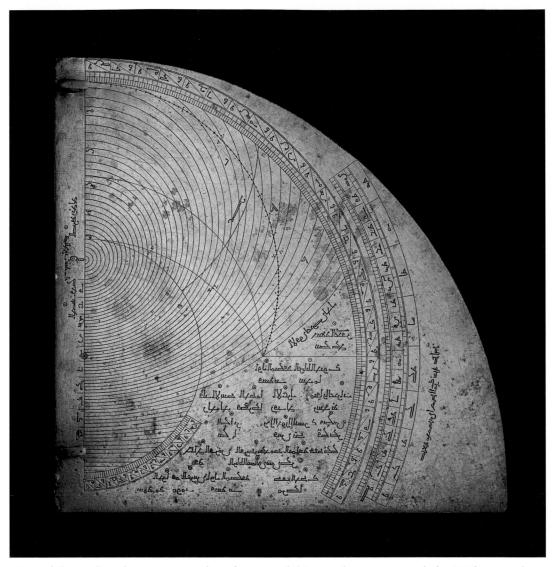

One of the earliest known examples of an astrolabic quadrant was made by Mohammad ibn Ahmad al-Mizzi in Damascus. The instrument combines geometry and trigonometry to resolve problems on spherical astronomy.

civilization [would] not [have been] able to rise and evolve without these numbers."[54]

Improvements in mathematics also helped geographers and astronomers, so these fields advanced rapidly during the Islamic golden age. The geographer al-Masudi, for example, turned out a widely read book that fairly accurately depicted central and western Asia, North Africa, and southern Europe.

Meanwhile, the astronomers of Caliph al-Mamun confirmed the figure

What Distinguished Humans from Animals

The fourteenth-century Muslim philosopher Ibn-Khaldun equated the arts and sciences with advanced civilization. People in his day understood that he was indirectly referring to and complimenting the Abbasids and other Muslim leaders whose wealth and encouragement of the arts and learning had made these refinements possible.

The crafts and sciences are the result of man's ability to think, through which he is distinguished from the animals. [The arts and sciences] come after the necessities. The [openness] of the [arts] to refinement, and the quality of [the purposes] they are to serve in view of the demands made by luxury and wealth, then correspond to the [level of] civilization of a given country.

Ibn-Khaldun. *The Muqaddimah: An Introduction to History.* Translated by Franz Rosenthal. Princeton, NJ: Princeton University Press, 1967, p. 347.

for earth's circumference that had been deduced by ancient Greek scientists. The thirteenth-century Muslim writer Ibn Khallikan recorded the clever manner in which the Muslim researchers accomplished this impressive feat. The ancient Greeks, he said, had found

that the circumference of the globe is 24,000 miles, or 8,000 farsakhs [since 1 farsakh equals 3 miles]. The caliph then said, "I wish you to [see] whether [that figure] is accurate or not." [On a spot on a level plain, the astronomers measured] the altitude of the Pole Star with certain instruments. They drove a peg into the ground and attached a long cord to it. They walked due north, [and] when the cord ran out, they stuck

another peg into the ground and fastened a cord to it, and carried on walking . . . until they reached a spot where the elevation of the Pole star had risen by one degree. Then they measured the distance they had traveled on the ground by means of the rope. The distance was $66^2/_3$ miles. Then they knew that every degree of the heavens was $66^2/_3$ miles on Earth. . . . They then multiplied the number of degrees of the heavens [360] by $66^2/_3$, [and] the total was 24,000 miles.[55]

Considering that the actual circumference of the earth is 24,902 miles (40,075km), this achievement, carried out using simple materials aided by pure mathematical logic, is striking.

Medicine and Optics

As some Muslim scientists advanced the disciplines of math and astronomy during the golden age, others made significant strides in medicine. Fred J. Hill and Nicholas Awde provide this thumbnail sketch of some of those strides:

Having translated the Greek classics on [medicine], Muslim scholars began to make their own unique contribution, expounding new theories and developing treatments that are astonishingly modern in their approach. . . . Muslim

An Italian translation of Ibn Sina's The Canon of Medicine *shows Ibn Sina and two disciples on the frontispiece of his masterwork on medicine.*

physicians routinely employed the practice of separating and isolating patients to avoid contagion. They developed sedatives and narcotic drugs to enable them to carry out operations, for which they invented hundreds of surgical instruments, employing animal intestines and silk to make sutures, and alcohol as an antiseptic [wound cleaner].[56]

Among these pioneering operations was the removal of cataracts, obstructions inside the eyes. This was done by sucking the unwanted material out through a hollow needle, a procedure that was not rediscovered in the West until 1846. In addition, medical researcher Ibn Sina (born 990) wrote a lengthy volume that listed all the medical knowledge accumulated by Muslim doctors up to his day. The book was later translated into several languages and used in European medical schools until the early 1600s. No less impressive was the work of Ibn Sina's contemporary, Spanish Muslim surgeon al-Zahrawi, who developed ways of treating ear infections, varicose veins, and dental problems. Al-Zahrawi was also the first doctor to describe hemophilia (a bleeding disorder) in detail and to recognize that it is hereditary.

Another important scientific pioneer, Alhazen (born 965), distinguished himself in optics, the study of the behavior of light. In fact, today even Western scientists view him as the "father" of that scientific discipline. Alhazen was the first person to demonstrate that Plato and other ancient thinkers had been wrong to say that people see objects because light exits the eyes and lands on those objects. Instead, he correctly stated, light is reflected off objects and then enters the eyes.

That Alhazen "demonstrated" this principle is a reference to his greatest contribution to science—one of the earliest scientific methods advocating conducting experiments to prove a theory or solve a problem. He said that one should first state the problem that needs solving, based on observation; then contrive a suggested solution; then test that solution by experimenting; then study and interpret the data produced by the experiments; and finally announce the solution, as derived from the earlier steps. This scientific method, conceived more than a thousand years ago, is nearly identical to the one used by modern researchers. In fact, this is no coincidence. In the 1100s some of Alhazen's texts became known in Europe, where they were translated into Latin and went on to strongly influence later European scientists.

Decorative Arts and Architecture

The Islamic empire's great cultural age was no less noteworthy for its achievements in the arts and architecture. "In contrast to Western art, in which painting and sculpture are dominant," two expert observers point out, "it is in the so-called decorative arts that Islamic art found its primary means of expression."[57] Among the decorative arts in which Muslim artisans excelled were

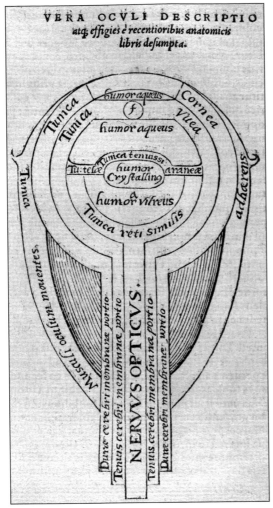

Alhuzen's drawing of the eye is from the 1572 Latin edition of his Opticae Thesaurus. *The book includes the first accurate descriptions of the parts of the eye and a scientific explanation of vision.*

ceramics (pottery), bronze-work, and glassmaking.

Muslim artisans also became experts at calligraphy, the art of creating beautiful handwritten words and symbols. These written elements were used to decorate a wide range of finely made crafts and other items, including pottery, metal objects, porcelain pieces, woodworking, architectural columns and doorjambs, coins, and handwritten books. Regarding the latter, Muslim artisans made some of the most attractive illuminated (illustrated) literary manuscripts of the medieval period. Not surprisingly, intricately illuminated versions of the Quran were widely popular throughout the Islamic lands.

In addition, calligraphy was used to adorn fine textiles, among the most beautiful of the Islamic decorative arts. According to Hill and Awde,

> Sometimes produced by imperial factories, [top-quality textiles] were used not only in homes, palaces, and mosques, but also served as gifts, rewards, and signs of political favor. The Muslim weavers adopted and developed the textile traditions of Sassanian Iran and the Mediterranean region [including Egypt]. The art of carpet-making was developed to a particularly high degree in Iran and Anatolia, where the need for protection against the winter cold made the carpets indispensable both in the shepherd's tent and in the prince's palace. In houses and palaces built of stone, brick, plaster, and glazed tile, carpets also provided a contrasting texture as floor and divan coverings and wall hangings.[58]

Meanwhile, to contain this wide array of craftwork and decoration, the Muslims developed their own distinctive

Mosques were the first distinctly Muslim buildings erected, and each one had a qibla *wall that faced Mecca.*

styles of architecture. Umayyad builders had made some advances toward this goal in the late 600s and early 700s. But it was under the Abbasids that Muslim architects began to make a major mark in erecting typically Islamic structures all the way from western Asia to Spain.

In part because of the Abbasid fascination for ancient Persia, these architects borrowed several ideas from Persian buildings. They also incorporated a few stylistic points from the Byzantines,

ancient Romans, and ancient Egyptians. What made the Islamic styles (which varied somewhat from region to region within the empire) unique was that they combined these older foreign elements with some fresh ones in ways that had never been seen before.

Among these fresh ideas were some used in the first distinctly Muslim buildings—mosques, where the faithful go to pray. Each mosque features a *qibla*, a wall specifically aligned to face Mecca.

Another feature that came to be used in most mosques was the minaret, a tall, slender tower in which the muezzin (the man who calls people to prayer) stands. Paul Lunde describes some more general architectural features of a majority of Islamic structures. There is a tendency, he says,

for all decoration to be highly stylized [exaggerated or abstract], geometric [based on squares, triangles, and other shapes], floral, or calligraphic, and [to employ continuously repeating visual themes]. Domes, often flattened, following the Byzantine model . . . became characteristic of Islamic architecture. Doors [and] windows . . . tend to be of great beauty, lovingly decorated and interesting in shape, whether in a palace or a simple house. Buildings both public and private are turned inward, with high defensive walls or heavily shuttered windows, to segregate the women [and] to protect the inhabitants in an unsettled world.[59]

Poets in Faraway Baghdad

Complementing the advances in science, the decorative arts, and architecture was an upsurge in well-conceived and elegantly executed literature. These written

The World's Most Poetic Cultures

Literature in the Islamic golden age was often dominated by poetry, which borrowed stylistically from earlier Persian poetry, as explained by researcher Michael H. Morgan.

Baghdad [grew] into the world capital of poetry. This [resulted] not only from the city's wealth, diversity, and inventiveness, [but also] from the fusion of two of the world's most poetic cultures and languages, Arabic and Persian. Both [had] already long held poetry to be the highest form of literary communication, and in Baghdad poetry [filled] the role that journalism and fiction [would] take up 1,300 years later. The leading poets of Baghdad . . . [lived] lives and [wrote] poems drenched in sex and drinking with a touch of blasphemy thrown in, [but at times rose] above the erotic and titillating [sexually arousing] to write of an exalted kind of romantic life, which experts see as the predecessor to later [poems] about courtly love.

Michael H. Morgan. *Lost History: The Enduring Legacy of Muslim Scientists, Thinkers, and Artists*. Washington, DC: National Geographic, 2007, p. 62.

works met a demand created by the rising numbers of people, particularly in the upper classes, who could read and write. Making the large-scale distribution of literature possible were new paper-making techniques, borrowed from China, which allowed Muslim artisans to fabricate a relatively low-cost form of paper.

Among the more popular literary forms was fanciful and/or romantic story-telling. The most famous example today is *The Book of One Thousand and One Nights* (of uncertain date), usually called *The Arabian Nights* in later English-language editions. A large collection of charming folktales and myths, it was compiled by numerous authors, mostly unknown, over the course of several centuries.

Even more admired by medieval Muslim readers was poetry. "In very broad terms," Hugh Kennedy remarks, "the early Abbasid caliphate [in the late 700s] was the age of poetry, when poetry and song were the most sought after and valued forms of cultural expression."[60] The poets frequently utilized styles and themes from earlier Persian verses, including friendship, love, and sex.

Very little Islamic poetry was translated and read by medieval Europeans.

Death Comes to All

Among the poets who flourished at the Abbasid court in Baghdad, one of the more original and skilled was Abu al-Atahiya, who lived from 748 to 825. He is best known for works that point out how brief and fleeting life and its pleasures are, including the following haunting verse.

Hereafter you shall see, shall see
Things hidden now from you, from you
In fullness of time you shall see
What makes the rest from the sleeper flee.
The rich and happy you shall see
Depart from hence to dust and dearth [absence]
In all that happens you shall see
The course of things eternally.

Quoted in Julia Ashtiany, ed. *Abbasid Belles-Letters. Cambridge History of Arabic Literature. Vol. 2* of Cambridge. Cambridge University Press, 1990, p. 289.

However, during the Abbasid period a growing number of European youths traveled to Islamic Spain to learn about Muslim astronomy and mathematics. "There is no doubt," say modern experts Judith M. Bennett and C. Warren Hollister, "that the intellectual development of medieval Europe was profoundly stimulated by the richness of Islamic libraries and the wisdom of their scholars."[62] Europe's subsequent cultural development would therefore have been very different had it not been for a group of far-thinking individuals in faraway, seemingly exotic Baghdad, then the world's most cultured city.

Epilogue

Later Islamic Dynasties and Empires

Between 750 and the early 1200s, various rival Muslim groups broke away from or overran Abbasid lands and set up their own states. In this way, the enormous Islamic Empire created by the immediate successors of Muhammad steadily shrank in size. Then the Mongol onslaught reduced large portions of the Middle East to ruin. In addition, the culturally splendid Islamic state in Spain fell in the 1400s to Christian armies (commanded by Queen Isabella of the Spanish kingdom of Castile and King Ferdinand of the Spanish kingdom of Aragon). Nearly everywhere, it seemed, Islamic civilization was threatened.

Fortunately for Islam and its adherents, however, both the faith and some Muslim-controlled lands survived these ravages. Although in the West Islam was never able to regain Spain, in the East several successful Islamic states and empires rose from the ashes of the Mongol incursions. A succession of these realms themselves came and went over the centuries. But one—the long-lived Ottoman Empire—survived into the twentieth century, when most of its territory was subdivided into a number of Muslim nations that still exist.

The Mamluks and Timurids

The complex post-Mongol succession of Islamic realms began with the Ayyubids, the dynasty founded by the talented and urbane Muslim leader Saladin in the 1170s. A few pockets of Ayyubid power managed to survive the Mongol invasion in various corners of the Middle East. These steadily fell to stronger Islamic groups in the 1300s and 1400s. More important, however, several years before the Mongols arrived on the scene the Ayyubid rulers had turned over their military affairs to a group of their subjects known as the Mamluks.

The term *mamluk* means "possessed" in Arabic. This reflects the fact that the Mamluks started out as young, foreign-born male slaves in the lands ruled by the Abbasids and other Islamic dynasties. These slaves converted to Islam and over time received extensive military training, making them valuable assets in Muslim armies. They became so numerous and trusted in Egypt that the Ayyubids made them their protectors. This turned out to be a wise decision because when the fearsome Mongols swept into the Middle East, they met their match in

Mamluks were former slaves converted to Islam who received extensive military training. They became an integral part of Muslim armies.

the Egyptian Mamluks. The latter handed the invaders a crushing defeat in 1260 (the first defeat the Mongols had ever experienced). This is why the Mongols were unable to continue their conquests into North Africa.

The Mamluks remained in power in Egypt until 1517. In the meantime, another group from central Asia, this one composed of devout Muslims, had assaulted the Middle East. It was led by Timur, a member of a Mongol tribe that had converted to Islam. In 1380 he gathered various Mongols, Turks, and others and invaded India, Russia, and large sections of the Middle East. Timur's successors, known as the Timurids, ruled Afghanistan, Iran, Armenia, and parts of Iraq until 1526. Most of these leaders were considerably more educated and constructive than Timur had been and avidly supported science and the arts.

Rise and Fall of the Ottomans

At the same time that the Mamluks were in charge of Egypt and the Timurids absorbed Iran and other Middle Eastern lands, a power that would eventually overcome them both was taking root in Anatolia, the future nation of Turkey. Not long after the Mongol invasion, several small Turkish Muslim states arose there. Most did not last long. But one, established by an ambitious man named Osman in 1299, became increasingly successful. Called Osmanli after its founder, a term that came into English as Ottoman, it proceeded to conquer most of the Balkans, including Greece, and seized

the rest of Anatolia from the Byzantines.

The Ottomans' initial main goal was to capture the Byzantine capital of Constantinople, the last major vestige of the ancient Roman Empire. Thanks to newly developed cannon technology they had acquired from Europe, they were able to bring about this watershed historical event in 1453. The great eighteenth-century English historian Edward Gibbon dramatically describes the city's downfall, writing,

> The Turks assaulted the city by sea and land [and] the cries of fear and of pain were drowned [out by] the martial music of drums [and] trumpets. . . . The Ottoman artillery thundered on all sides; and the . . . Greeks and the Turks were [engulfed] in a cloud of smoke, which could only be dispelled by the final deliverance or destruction of the Roman Empire. . . . [At last, the city's] double walls were reduced by the cannons to a heap of ruins [and] after a siege of fifty-three days, that Constantinople which had defied the power of [numerous enemies over the centuries], was trampled in the dust.[63]

The Ottoman realm continued to expand, and at its height in the late 1600s it encompassed North Africa (including Egypt), western Arabia, Palestine, and Iraq, as well as Anatolia and the Balkans. Although large, this amounted to considerably less than half the extent of the medieval Islamic Empire at its own zenith. A number of Ottoman rulers dreamed of restoring that vast past domain's former glories. But their dream was never fulfilled. Between 1683 and 1718 the Ottomans relentlessly tried but failed to conquer eastern Europe, campaigns that exhausted their armies and left them open to attacks by their foes. Later in the 1700s Europe took back major portions of the Balkans and Russia overran the northern sectors of the Ottoman realm.

Although their territorial possessions steadily shrank, the Ottoman rulers were able to hold onto power until they and their allies, the Germans, were decisively defeated in the climax of World War I (1914–1918). The last Islamic empire was then divided among the victors, the British, French, and Russians. (The fourth major winner of the war, the United States, made no territorial claims on the Ottomans.)

A Safer, More Peaceful World

In the decades that followed, nearly forty nations arose on former Ottoman lands, most of them inhabited by Muslims. Including Saudi Arabia, Yemen, Iraq, Syria, Lebanon, and Turkey to name only a few, most came to be ruled by dictators. Many of the peoples of these lands still recognize their spiritual roots in the medieval Islamic Empire and look back on its successes and accomplishments with a touch of awe. The members of a few extremist groups, like Osama bin Laden's infamous al Qaeda, continue to long for the restoration of that Caliphate of old. However, a majority of Muslims are more interested in making their individual modern nations successful and leading fulfilling lives within them. They know that creating empires at the expense of one's neighbors—called imperialism—is no longer accepted in the world.

In fact, most Muslims would like to live under peaceful democratic governments, not aggressive imperial ones. This was clearly shown in the huge demonstrations staged early in 2011 by the inhabitants of Egypt, Tunisia, Yemen, Libya, and other Muslim countries. In all cases, the cries of the protesters were for an end to dictators and the establishment of freedom and democratic systems. Indeed, Fred J. Hill and Nicholas Awde point out, "the overwhelming majority of Muslims will argue that their religion is not incompatible with the principles of democracy, especially the idea that the voice of the people should be heard and acted upon, and that people have the right to choose their leaders."[64]

Media interviews with many of the demonstrators revealed how they view the future. Several of them stated that they look forward to the day when democracy is as common in their countries as it is now in the West. Along with a majority of Westerners, they hope that this will remove the last shreds of the barriers of misunderstanding and mistrust that stood between medieval Europe and the medieval Islamic Empire. The mutual expectation is that such developments will ultimately bring about a safer and more peaceful world.

Notes

Introduction: Dreams of Empires Lost

1. Efraim Karsh. *Islamic Imperialism: A History*. New Haven, CT: Yale University Press, 2006, p. 230.
2. Quoted in Tom O'Connor. "Religious Zealotry and Terrorism." www.drtomoconnor.com/3400/3400lect04.htm.
3. John Bar Penkaye. *Summary of World History*. Translated by Sebastian Brock. The Tertullian Project. www.tertullian.org/fathers/john_bar_penkaye_history_15_trans.htm.

Chapter One: Muhammad and His Struggles

4. Fred J. Hill and Nicholas Awde. *A History of the Islamic World*. New York: Hippocrene, 2003, pp. 19–20.
5. Richard Hooker. "Pre-Islamic Arabic Culture." Washington State University. http://wsu.edu/~dee/ISLAM/PRE.HTM.
6. Alfred Guillaume. *Islam*. New York: Penguin, 1990, p. 5.
7. Guillaume. *Islam*, pp. 28–29.
8. Quran 33:40.
9. Karsh. *Islamic Imperialism*, p. 11.
10. Karsh. *Islamic Imperialism*, p. 11.
11. W. H. McNeill. *The Rise of the West: A History of the Human Community*. Chicago: University of Chicago Press, 1992, pp. 464–465.

12. David Nicolle. *The Great Islamic Conquests, A.D. 632–750*. Oxford: Osprey, 2009, p. 18.

Chapter Two: The Early Muslim Conquests

13. Quran 9:13–14; 9:5.
14. James E. Lindsay. *Daily Life in the Medieval Islamic World*. Westport, CT: Greenwood, 2005, p. 59.
15. Quoted in Barnaby Rogerson. *The Heirs of Muhammad: Islam's First Century and the Origins of the Sunni-Shia Split*. New York: Overlook, 2006, pp. 32–33.
16. Albert Hourani. *A History of the Arab Peoples*. New York: Grand Central, 1991, p. 22.
17. Quoted in Bernard Lewis, ed. and trans. *Islam, from the Prophet Muhammad to the Capture of Constantinople*. Vol. 1. New York: Oxford University Press, 1987, p. 5.
18. Quoted in Lewis. *Islam, Vol. 1*, pp. 5–6.
19. Theodor Noeldeke. *Sketches from Eastern History*. London: Adam and Charles Black, 1892, p. 73.
20. Karsh. *Islamic Imperialism*, pp. 22–23.
21. Hugh Kennedy. *The Great Arab Conquests: How the Spread of Islam Changed the World We Live In*. Cambridge, MA: Da Capo, 2008, pp. 84–85.

22. Hourani. *A History of the Arab Peoples*, p. 24.
23. Nicolle. *The Great Islamic Conquests, A.D. 632–750*, pp. 7–8.
24. Quoted in Lewis. *Islam*, p. 7.
25. Rogerson. *The Heirs of Muhammad*, p. 283.

Chapter Three: Islam Rocked by Civil Strife

26. Paul Lunde. *Islam: Faith, Culture, History*. New York: Dorling Kindersley, 2002, p. 50.
27. Fred M. Donner. "Muhammad and the Caliphate." In *The Oxford History of Islam*, edited by John L. Esposito. New York: Oxford University Press, 1999, p. 15.
28. Rogerson. *The Heirs of Muhammad*, p. 294.
29. Rogerson. *The Heirs of Muhammad*, pp. 296–297.
30. Quoted in Rogerson. *The Heirs of Muhammad*, p. 298.
31. Ali ibn Abi Talib. *Najh ul Balagha*. www.nahjulbalagha.org/Letter Detail.php?Letter=53.
32. Quran 17:33.
33. Quoted in Rogerson. *The Heirs of Muhammad*, p. 308.
34. Amira K. Bennison. *The Great Caliphs: The Golden Age of the Abbasid Empire*. New Haven, CT: Yale University Press, 2009, p. 17.
35. Quoted in Marven Gettleman and Stuart Schaar, eds. *The Middle East and Islamic World Reader*. New York: Grove, 2003, p. 25.

Chapter Four: A New Burst of Expansion

36. Bernard Lewis. *The Middle East: A Brief History of the Last 2,000 Years.* New York: Scribner, 1995, pp. 65–66.
37. Lewis. *The Middle East*, p. 67.
38. Quoted in Lindsay. *Daily Life in the Medieval Islamic World*, p. 67.
39. Quoted in Leon Bernard and Theodore B. Hodges, eds. *Readings in European History*. New York: Macmillan, 1958, p. 85.

Chapter Five: Baghdad and Its Challengers

40. Judith M. Bennett and C. Warren Hollister. *Medieval Europe: A Short History*. New York: McGraw-Hill, 2006, p. 89.
41. Lunde. *Islam*, p. 54.
42. Bennison. *The Great Caliphs*, p. 102.
43. Lewis. *The Middle East*, p. 83.
44. Quoted in Norton Downs, ed. *Basic Documents in Medieval History*. Melbourne, FL: Krieger, 1992, pp. 74–75.
45. Quoted in Bernard and Hodges. *Readings in European History*, pp. 103–104.
46. Karsh. *Islamic Imperialism*, p. 83.
47. Bernard Lewis. *The Assassins*. New York: Basic Books, 2003, pp. xi–xii.
48. Quoted in Gettleman and Schaar. *The Middle East and Islamic World Reader*, p. 50.
49. Guillaume. *Islam*, p. 86.

Chapter Six: Islamic Culture's Golden Age

50. Quoted in Bernard Lewis. *The Muslim Discovery of Europe*. New York: Norton, 2001, p. 139.
51. Quoted in Hourani. *A History of the Arab Peoples*, p. 76.
52. Ahmad Dallal. "Science, Medicine, and Technology: The Making of a

Scientific Culture." In *The Oxford History of Islam*, p. 155.

53. Michael H. Morgan. *Lost History: The Enduring Legacy of Muslim Scientists, Thinkers, and Artists*. Washington, DC: National Geographic, 2007, p. 89.

54. Morgan. *Lost History*, p. 89.

55. Quoted in Hugh Kennedy. *When Baghdad Ruled the Muslim World: The Rise and Fall of Islam's Greatest Dynasty*. Cambridge, MA: Da Capo, 2005, pp. 258–259.

56. Hill and Awde. *A History of the Islamic World*, p. 56.

57. Hill and Awde. *A History of the Islamic World*, p. 64.

58. Hill and Awde. *A History of the Islamic World*, p. 65.

59. Lunde. *Islam*, p. 86.

60. Kennedy. *When Baghdad Ruled the Muslim World*, p. 113.

61. Quoted in Morgan. *Lost History*, p. 62.

62. Bennett and Hollister. *Medieval Europe*, p. 94.

Epilogue: Later Islamic Dynasties and Empires

63. Edward Gibbon. *The Decline and Fall of the Roman Empire*. Vol. 3. Edited by David Womersley. New York: Penguin, 1994, pp. 960–963.

64. Hill and Awde. *A History of the Islamic World*, p. 204.

For More Information

Books

Karen Armstrong. *Islam: A Short History*. New York: Modern Library, 2000. A leading expert on religions and their history, Armstrong tells a complex story in a straightforward, understandable manner.

Reza Aslan. *No God but God: The Origins, Evolution, and Future of Islam*. New York: Random House, 2005. A respected expert on Islam has produced a thoughtful examination of the faith and its history and ideas.

Amira K. Bennison. *The Great Caliphs: The Golden Age of the Abbasid Empire*. New Haven, CT: Yale University Press, 2009. This well-researched, well-written volume brings the great age of the Abbasids to life.

Anne Blanchard and Emmanuel Cerisier. *Arab Science and Invention in the Golden Age*. New York: Enchanted Lion, 2008. Aimed at younger readers, this handsome book contains numerous colorful original drawings, along with a well-written text.

Marvin E. Gettleman and Stuart Schaar, eds. *The Middle East and Islamic World Reader*. New York: Grove, 2003. This anthology contains numerous original documents pertaining to the rise and expansion of Islam.

Lesley Hazleton. *After the Prophet: The Epic Story of the Shia-Sunni Split in Islam*. New York: Doubleday, 2009. A sweeping look at the reasons for the division of Islam into opposing factions.

Marshall G. S. Hodgson. *The Venture of Islam. Vol. 1, The Classical Age of Islam*. Chicago: University of Chicago Press, 1977. Hodgson's multivolume study is universally recognized as one of the leading works on Islamic history.

Marshall G. S. Hodgson. *The Venture of Islam. Vol. 2, The Expansion of Islam in the Middle Periods*. Chicago: University of Chicago Press, 1977.

Brendan January. *The Arab Conquests in the Middle East*. Minneapolis: Twenty-First Century, 2009. Aimed at junior high and high school readers, this colorfully illustrated book summarizes the expansion of Muslim peoples in the centuries following the birth of Islam.

Efraim Karsh. *Islamic Imperialism: A History*. New Haven, CT: Yale University Press, 2006. A useful overview of the great Islamic conquests and the societies they created, this volume takes the reader all the way up to the twentieth century.

Hugh Kennedy. *The Great Arab Conquests: How the Spread of Islam Changed the World We Live In*. Cambridge, MA: Da Capo, 2008. Kennedy, a distinguished

Scottish scholar, examines the rise and fall of the medieval Islamic empires.

Bernard Lewis. *The Arabs in History*. New York: Oxford University Press, 2002. A classic book by one of the world's leading authorities on Islam.

Bernard Lewis. *The Assassins*. New York: Basic Books, 2003. In another excellent volume, Lewis traces the rise and fall of this radical, murderous medieval Islamic sect.

James E. Lindsay. *Daily Life in the Medieval Islamic World*. Westport, CT: Greenwood, 2005. The author skillfully captures numerous aspects of life in one of the great medieval civilizations.

Paul Lunde. *Islam: Faith, Culture, History*. New York: Dorling Kindersley, 2002. A well-written synopsis of Islamic culture and history that is both nicely illustrated and easy to read.

Seyyed H. Nasr. *Islam: Religion, History, and Civilization*. New York: HarperOne, 2002. Nasr, a noted Islamic scholar, delivers an accurate introduction to the subject that does not overwhelm unfamiliar readers with too much in-depth information.

David Nicolle. *The Great Islamic Conquests, A.D. 632–750*. Oxford: Osprey, 2009. A brief but excellent introduction to the subject, with numerous appropriate and informational illustrations.

Malise Ruthven. *Historical Atlas of Islam*. Cambridge, MA: Harvard University Press, 2004. An excellent and useful collection of maps, along with colorful drawings, relating to the expansion of Islam over the centuries.

Tamara Sonn. *A Brief History of Islam*. Malden, MA: Blackwell, 2010. A concise, easy-to-read overview of the subject written by a respected professor, this will appeal to younger and older readers alike.

Richard Spilsbury and Louise Spilsbury. *The Islamic Empires*. Chicago: Raintree, 2007. Written for students, this easy-to-read volume introduces the major Islamic dynasties and realms over the centuries.

Christopher Tyerman. *The Crusades*. New York: Oxford University Press, 2004. A brief but informative overview of the Crusades by one of the foremost historians specializing in that topic.

Websites

Baghdad Under the Abbasids (www .fordham.edu/halsall/source/ 1000baghdad.html). A valuable primary source depicting that great city in its prime.

The Battle of Yarmouk (www.fordham .edu/halsall/source/yarmuk.html). This medieval account describes one of the pivotal battles during the early expansion of the Islamic Empire.

The Golden Age of Islam (www.irfi .org/articles/articles_401_450/gold en_age_of_islam.htm). This article by Zachariah Matthews tells some of the highlights of one of history's greatest cultural outbursts.

The Holy Quran (http://quod.lib.um ich.edu/k/koran/browse.html). A widely read translation by M. H. Shakir of Islam's holiest book.

Ibn Alhazen (www.trincoll.edu/depts/ phil/philo/phils/muslim/alhazen. html). A brief but informative biography of one of the most brilliant scientists of the medieval world.

Islamic Architecture (http://gallery .sjsu.edu/islamictutorial). In this useful site, clicking on "Timeline" on the second page leads to pictures and written descriptions of some of the world's most famous Islamic structures.

Islamic Spain (http://explorethemed .com/reconquista.asp?c=1). A helpful overview of Muslim civilization that existed in Spain from the 700s to the 1400s.

The Life of Muhammad (www.pbs.org/ muhammad/timeline_html.shtml). PBS provides this well-mounted short biography of Islam's founder.

Index

Picture Credits

About the Author

In addition to his acclaimed volumes on the ancient world, historian Don Nardo has produced several studies of medieval times, including *Medieval Europe*, *The Scientific Revolution*, *Life on a Medieval Pilgrimage*, *The Italian Renaissance*, *The Vikings*, and biographies of late medieval astronomers Tycho Brahe and Galileo. Nardo resides with his wife Christine in Massachusetts.